Desert Wood

WESTERN LITERATURE SERIES

Western Trails: A Collection of Short Stories by Mary Austin
selected and edited by Melody Graulich

Cactus Thorn
by Mary Austin with foreword and afterword by Melody Graulich

Dan De Quille, the Washoe Giant: A Biography and Anthology
prepared by Richard A. Dwyer and Richard E. Lingenfelter

Desert Wood: An Anthology of Nevada Poets
edited by Shaun T. Griffin

Western Literature Series

Desert Wood

An Anthology of Nevada Poets

Edited by Shaun T. Griffin

Foreword by Richard Shelton

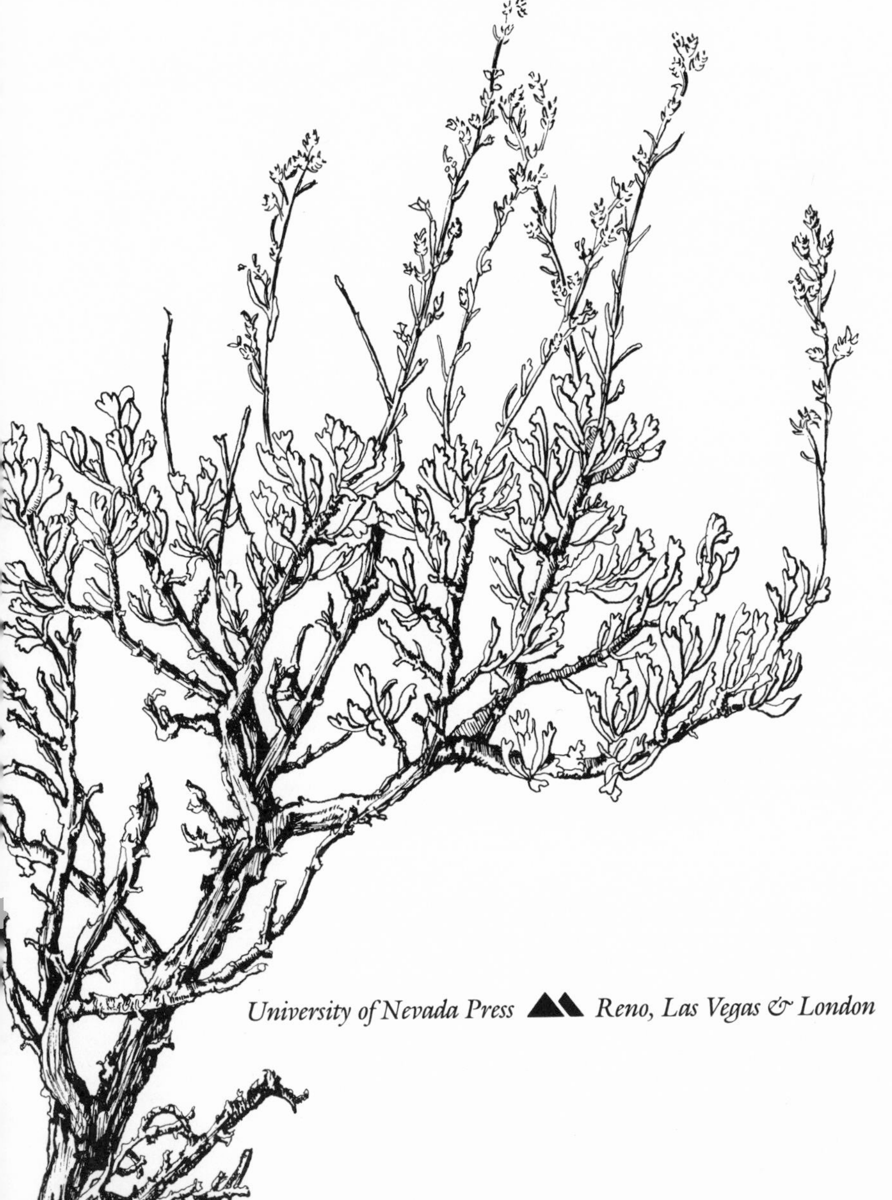

University of Nevada Press ▲▲ *Reno, Las Vegas & London*

Western Literature Series Editor:
John H. Irsfeld
The paper used in this book meets the requirement of American National Standard for Information Sciences—ANSI Z39.48-1984. Binding materials were chosen for strength and durability.

Title page illustration: Dwarf sagebrush (*Artemisia arbuscula*), by Christine Stetter.

Library of Congress
Cataloging-in-Publication Data
Desert wood : an anthology of Nevada poets / edited by Shaun T. Griffin ; foreword by Richard Shelton.
p. cm. — (Western literature series)
Includes bibliographical references and index.
ISBN 0-87417-175-X (cloth ed. : alk. paper)
ISBN 0-87417-181-4 (paper ed. : alk. paper)
1. American poetry—Nevada. 2. Nevada—Poetry. I. Griffin, Shaun T. (Shaun Timothy), 1953– . II. Series.
PS571.N3D47 1991
811'.540809793–dc20 91-3952
CIP

University of Nevada Press,
Reno, Nevada 89557 USA

Designed by Richard Hendel
Printed in the United States of America

9 8 7 6 5 4 3 2 1

for

Helen "Zeke" Modarelli

poet, friend, Nevadan

1904–1990

Yet whatever else an anthologist may be, he is a worker in time, a kind of historian. His aim is the present, but his material is the past; and the farther back he looks the deeper he sees.

HAYDEN CARRUTH

Contents

Foreword

This is my letter to the World
That never wrote to Me
—Emily Dickinson

It might seem strange to compare the poetry in this anthology to the poetry of Emily Dickinson, but that is the comparison I often thought of as I read these poems, in spite of the fact that a mental picture of Emily Dickinson in Las Vegas is probably the most surreal image that has ever entered my mind, or is likely to. But the comparison persisted. Some of the poems in this anthology have the desperate quality of messages found in bottles far out at sea, and others have a dogged grandeur like Emily's letter to a world which had not written to her and would not, in her lifetime, respond.

I am not suggesting that all poets in Nevada write from isolated ranches hundreds of miles from civilization. Many of them actually live in or near one of Nevada's two large population centers, Reno and Las Vegas. But most of them write from a deep sense of isolation, as Emily did, and their work reflects it. Neither was Emily a miniaturist, as some people who have only a slight acquaintance with her poetry assume. She painted with broad strokes and in rich colors, and with a kind of authority which comes from complete assurance, the assurance of all she had given up. In this, too, many of the poems here remind me of her work.

The poets represented in this anthology have come to know several kinds of isolation. (I am reminded that years ago I was writing a short prose piece and groping for an image of physical, social, and spiritual isolation. I came up with Ely, Nevada, and titled the piece "Doing Without.") Nevada is virtually all desert. Its mountains are islands surrounded by a sea of desert, and in them many kinds of flora and fauna have evolved in isolation and are quite different from their relatives elsewhere. The color of the map tells us more about the physical isolation Nevada demands of its residents than does the geographical location of the state.

But there is a different kind of record which suggests another kind of isolation for Nevada's poets, and it was a kind Emily Dickinson knew and suffered from. I am referring to the track record of publications by Nevada poets and the national recognition they have received. It is a bleak record. Only one Nevada poet has ever been awarded a National Endowment for the Arts writer's fellowship. Over the years, few of them have published with major eastern presses. Many of them are almost completely unknown outside of Nevada. Emily knew the same kind of treatment. She was isolated from the world of publication largely because she was a woman—and an innovative one at that. Her isolation was deliberately imposed from without and generally accepted by the society of her day; and while she grew increasingly reclusive in regard to that society, she did not turn away from her craft. She focused on it until she had ground the bitter provender of isolation and neglect into a kind of triumph, her own personal triumph. She continued to write her letters to the world, expecting no reply, no acknowledgment. And so do the poets of Nevada.

It is curious that while Emily Dickinson wrote much of her best work during the Civil War—in the midst of which Nevada was rushed into statehood because the Union needed its silver and its votes—she never, in her poems, mentions that war by name nor ever refers to any specific battle in it, although the newspapers of the day were filled with detailed accounts of combat, and even New Englanders talked of little else. And yet, probably about two years before that war began, she had written, prophetically it would seem, one of the best poems ever written about war, and certainly one of the best accounts of the defeated Confederacy and the desolated South. It was, not coincidentally, also a poem about her own situation.

Not one of all the purple Host
Who took the Flag today
Can tell the definition
So clear of Victory

As he defeated—dying—
On whose forbidden ear
The distant strains of triumph
Burst agonized and clear!

No soldier who took part in the Civil War, and not even Walt Whitman, who worked with the human wreckage it created, captured the essence of that struggle better. It took a lonely spinster, isolated from the war and even from much of the daily life around her, to distill the entire tragedy into eight searing, unforgettable lines.

I am suggesting that isolation, even today, has its rewards for a poet, especially if it is seen for what it is, embraced, and nurtured, although those rewards do not usually include immediate recognition. I think a poet requires a sense of isolation from the thing seen in order to see it clearly, in order to digest and distill it. Isolation does not mean indifference or ignorance. But it gives the poet some ground to stand on, a place from which to view the world without being overcome by it. Emily became a recluse, but the words "windows," "light," and "sky" keep appearing in her poetry, as well as references to enormous distances and stretches of time. "Infinity" became almost her private garden, something she did not fear.

In regard to isolation created by great distances and a desert world which seems timeless, the Nevada poets in this anthology, as William Carlos Williams said, "have it over a troop / of artists." Nevada poets "have the ground sense necessary." They write about various kinds of deserts—physical and spiritual and somewhere between the two—the everyday desert of boredom, frustration, and despair, the one we all have some experience with. They do not, generally, write about some of the things that less isolated poets in the eastern part of the country often write about, and I find that interesting. Nevada poets do not often write about paintings, especially French paintings. They have little to say about foreign films. Nor do they seem to be overly concerned with sex and sexual experimentation, something which fascinates their counterparts in some other sections of the country. They have a clearly defined sense of the individual and a marked feeling for landscape, whether it is downtown Reno or the shimmering desert highway—"100 miles and not one tree."

Above all, they have a strong sense of their own isolation, not only their isolation from people in other places, but their isolation within their own landscape. They do not belong to the world of the casinos, a world which I believe lies at the heart of Las Vegas and even Reno. Yet the poets cannot survive in the surrounding desert without the necessities provided by the towns and cities. And so they exist in the margins, on the edge of things, hemmed in by two different kinds of wilderness, one physical and one cultural. They are, in effect, frontier poets.

One can hardly think of the American frontier without thinking of the historian Frederick Jackson Turner, who defined it as "the meeting point between savagery and civilization." (Isn't that an apt description of Las Vegas?) But a whole generation of recent western historians have challenged Turner's view of a single, monolithic frontier which ceased to exist when the West was closed to further homesteading. They contend that there were many frontiers in the West, often overlapping, and that some of them continue to exist today.

Surely the embattled line of troops who represent the cultural life of Nevada and struggle under the banners of education and art exist on a frontier and are themselves a frontier. And although that frontier includes many intellectuals, teachers, writers, and artists, it is very thin, barely a veneer when seen in the context of the total population and the state's economy. It manages to exist somehow, but how do poets survive as part of that frontier? Barely, if at all. "It would have starved a Gnat— / To live so small as I—," said Emily. I think the Nevada poets would agree. Although they live on the edge of expansive vistas of beautiful desert and mountains, they live in the straitened circumstances and limitations demanded by a frontier.

I think the poetry in this anthology should be considered within the framework of "frontier literature," and there is no hint of the pejorative or patronizing in that label. The moment Emily Dickinson attempted to have any of her poems published, she stepped, as a woman, onto a frontier, the cutting edge of her society, and it cut her badly. I, too, am a frontier poet if I'm any kind of poet at all. I was born and raised just across the Nevada border in Idaho, which some easterners still refer to as "Iowa," while true New Englanders confuse it with Ohio. I'm very proud of being a frontier poet, and especially proud of being a native frontier poet.

So I take my stand with the poets in this anthology at "the meeting point between savagery and civilization." It's not the safest nor most comfortable place for a poet, but in one sense or another it is where all real poets in America live. It offers us a marginal existence as poets, but far less marginal than Emily Dickinson's frontier offered her, and her inner life was deep and rich beyond all reckoning. And today, as our nation prepares for another savage war in the name of civilization, I cannot even dare to hope that life will be easy for the Nevada poets, but I can hope that their work survives and continues to remind us all of the frontiers we live on.

Richard Shelton
Tucson, Arizona
30 September 1990

Preface

Years ago when I first came to Nevada, a good friend of mine was publishing *The Nevada Poet*. I still have a copy of that ill-fated anthology and I think of it as the predecessor to this book. In fact, were it not for the hard work of the editors, Roger Smith and Gary Short, I doubt the seeds for such an anthology would exist today. Many things have changed in the interim. Most notable is the great influx of poets into the state, whose range of styles and emotions is one of this book's virtues (if such things can be said by an editor). And I was not prepared for the raw talent that is rooted here. Many poets came to my attention by hook and crook, and over the years I have watched their work mature and marveled at its freshness.

I think of the small sheaf of poems that arrived in the mail with a Tonopah postmark. Yes, Tonopah. I opened them to find the work of a former beat cop from L.A. and San Francisco, Ronald Manning, who is now the graveyard weather watcher for the Tonopah Airport. Inside the envelope were six of the most enchanting narrative poems I'd read in months. By his own admission, Manning is a novelist at heart, but he couldn't stay away from poetry. I think also of the joyfully understated Sun Valley woman, Milly Brown, who was Josephine Mile's personal assistant at Berkeley for two years and a widely published poet in her own right before, in her words, "life intervened."

Moreover, there are the treasures of translation: an exiled Chilean poet, Emma Sepúlveda, with two books published in Spain, but not a word translated into English—until now. There is no steering away from her words. Though dark with war, they rise above all else to transcend borders, transcend fear. And imagine my joy at receiving a book of poetry from the only poet in the state to have received a National Endowment for the Arts Fellowship in Creative Writing, Stephen Liu. His poems—contemplative, thoughtful, with a presence all their own in English—took him one year to translate into Mandarin.

Included, as well, are the English teachers, north, south, and east: Tom Meschery, Joan Cutuly, Bobbi Curry-Cartwright, Robert McGinty, and Kelly Moon. They do not work in universities, but in high schools, teaching poetry often in an atmosphere of dislike and distrust. (I wish I could recount the number of English teachers who have confided in me that they were afraid to teach poetry, or taught it last, or not at all, because it appeared to be so difficult a subject to teach.)

There were countless letters from young writers, all hoping to be included and proudly claiming their heritage in the scheme of things. I could go on with more such anecdotes, but the end result was that I learned poetry is alive in this state, very much alive. Faced with the publication of anthologies from most of the neighboring states, I wondered if Nevada's poetry would stack up. In my opinion, it does, though this book has decidedly different expectations than some. The predominant criteria for consideration was a strong Nevada connection, be it birth, residence, or lasting faith in things otherwise referred to as "Nevadan." Passing through didn't count, nor did wanting to pass through. As to inclusion, the primary criteria was "poetry that took my head off," to paraphrase Emily Dickinson. A conscious decision was made to not include cowboy poetry, since two anthologies have recently been published whose focus was cowboy poetry. And I also wanted the book to be more than a Las Vegas/Reno literary guide. I received poems from more than fifty towns in this state, but still I fear all of the good poets are not included. Likewise, I wanted the book to truly represent *all* Nevadans. Lofty expectations.

There were other limitations to be faced: the period of time covered by the anthology, the length, and the cost. But what book is not bound by such things? This is a contemporary anthology, roughly dating from the 1930s onward, a time when there was a flourishing literary community in Reno and Virginia City. In the mid 1940s Joanne de Longchamps, Walter Clark, Thelma "Brownie" Ireland, Harold Witt, and Irene Bruce were writing and publishing much of Nevada's lasting poetry of the period. But as I remarked to a colleague, some of them would go on to suffer a kind of benign neglect. Irene Bruce was paid $100 for publication of her poems in *The Nevada Poet*. At the time, she told Gary Short it was the most money she had ever received for her poems in her lifetime, and she was then nearly eighty. The fact that Joanne de Longchamps died relatively unknown outside of Nevada makes one wonder what an address has to do with literature. In her case, it spelled isolation from her peers and, ultimately, a beautiful and unrelenting poet coming to her end waging silence. Of course, Walter Clark went on to achieve prominence for his fiction, but he was the exception. Many poets have gone to their graves in obscurity. This book seeks to right that wrong. These poets are included here because their work warrants consideration today—maybe now more than ever—

especially Harold Witt and "Brownie" Ireland who continue to write to this day.

There is a story, a human story, in the work of every poet between these covers. If I had to give just one word to their stories, it would be survival. I think of Judy Carlisle, mother of seven, living most of her years on a minimum-wage job, but writing poems that dazzle. Bill Wilborn's book, *Rooms*, was seventeen years in the making. Survival, or just plain tenacity? I don't know. I do know that these poets have worked for every word in this book: Billie Jean James was twice a finalist for the Walt Whitman Award; Wil Stevens, founding editor of *Interim*, published Carolyn Kizer's first poem when she was just seventeen years old; Adrian Louis, an enrolled member of the Lovelock Paiute Indian Tribe and now four books of poetry later, teaches in the *Fire Water World*; and Bill Fox and Kirk Robertson have been the backbone of small-press publishing in Reno and Fallon. They've survived, all of them, in a land commonly referred to as a "cultural wasteland."

Jim Huskey, after years of graduate school, finally returned to his poems —the only thing that calls a writer at forty is poetry. His are vivid poems. Who but Gary Short could give us the quiet evocations of a mill town blowing to dust when the smelter closes? There are more, many more that I have neglected here, all of whom count themselves among Nevada poets in the 1990s.

Nevada, in so many ways, is a state of contradictions. The late Irene Bruce died in abject poverty, yet just seven years later literary fellowships for $4,000 would be given to promising and accomplished writers. In just four short years, the Western Mountain Writers' Conference grew to attract over three hundred people with the likes of Carolyn Kizer and William Stafford presenting workshops. And after just two short issues, the *Comstock Quarterly* folded in the summer of 1989 without even a chance of succeeding.

Still, literary magazines manage to flourish: *Interim* in the south, resurrected from obscurity by its tireless editor, Wil Stevens; *Pegasus* founded and edited by Elizabeth Perry in Boulder City; *Bristlecone* in the north, which really started as a voice of the Ash Canyon Poets and until 1990 was a vital literary presence in northwestern Nevada. Though *West Coast Poetry Review* and *Scree*—two northern Nevada literary magazines of the 1970s and 1980s—have ceased publication, Bill Fox continues to operate West Coast Poetry Review Press, and Kirk Robertson still runs Duck

Down Press. Their books are highly crafted works of printing and art, which appeal to the reader long after publication. Bob Blesse has similarly picked up the baton from his predecessor at the Black Rock Press, Ken Carpenter. Under the new imprint, Rainshadow Editions, the press is producing fine hand-printed letterpress broadsides and short-run books. Doubtless there are numerous other such stories. Does all of this point to a literary renaissance in the state? Perhaps, in the drought and flood cycles of publishing we've grown accustomed to, yes. More than all of this, however, is the spirit of the Nevada poet that sings on from generation to generation. In the mid 1940s Irene Bruce, Harold Witt, Joanne de Longchamps, and others met to read their poetry in the Reno Poetry Workshop. And today, despite all manner of forces to the contrary, the Ash Canyon Poets of Carson City continue to meet weekly to read, write, and critique one another's work, producing some strong new voices in northwestern Nevada.

This book will ultimately be judged as a lens through which to view Nevada poets from the 1930s to the present. Despite every attempt to read and include all poems of quality from this period, I have little confidence that this has been accomplished. My motivation for editing this anthology was, at first, an undefined desire to see Nevada poets represented in more than passing form. But now, after nearly three thousand poems, countless books, manuscripts, anecdotal references, clippings, microfiche, libraries, and over two years of quiet recollection in their presence, it is because of the poetry itself that I edit this book. The poetry made the journey worth the coming home, home to the realization that Nevada poets large and small are a singularly powerful group. They matter to us now and to the future generations that will follow.

Many people have supported me throughout this project. My good friend, Robert Blesse, the head of special collections at the University of Nevada, Reno, first expressed interest in publishing this book in October 1988. The winter before, I met the editor of the *Comstock Chronicle*, Gary Elam, in a bookstore in Virginia City. This chance meeting led to my writing a poetry column for the paper. I had already met many of the poets in this book one by one, reading and rereading their material, in some cases over a period of ten years. But it was only when I began writing about them for the paper that I really began to learn about their work. Without the help of the state's twenty-eight newspapers and sixty-four libraries, I wouldn't have received the material I did. Many jewels were unearthed in the process (a 1928 Nevada poetry anthology sent to me from a curator at the Humboldt County Museum is one example).

This book is so much more than "Desert Wood," but there I must stop. I have come late to this body of poets, many of whose lifetimes were bordered in stanzas. For their sharing, I am grateful and more than a little proud. For over sixty years they have recorded the sun, sky, and sage that daily came without asking. Now I swing this cradle of voices to you.

A final note. Were it not for the early encouragement of my own work, I would never have tried to collect under one cover the work of so many others. Thank you to many people—poets, friends, and family. Your influence and your patience has stayed with me through the long nights of revision and editing. And if she were a more public poet, the last credit would go to my wife, Debby.

So I end where I started—in homage to a body of literature larger than I am capable of appreciating. If the lens of literature is ever to change, then let it begin here, in the Western states with such promise as these writers hold.

Shaun T. Griffin
Virginia City, Nevada
October 1990

Acknowledgments

For permission to reprint all works in this volume by each of the following poets, grateful acknowledgment is made to the holders of copyright, publishers, or representatives named below and on the following pages, which constitute an extension of the copyright page.

"Autumn Oak," "Haiku," by Thelma "Brownie" Ireland. From *The Chapparal Poet* and *International Haiku Magazine*. Copyright 1975 by Thelma Ireland and reprinted with her permission.

"Virginia City, Nevada," "Sea Rose," "Rattle Snake," "Arrowhead," by Irene Bruce. From *Crag and Sand* and *Night Cry*. Copyright 1945 and 1950 by Reno Silver State Press and Reno Poetry West. Reprinted by permission of the author.

"Resignation," by Helen "Zeke" Modarelli. From the *Comstock Chronicle*, 1988. Copyright 1982 Helen "Zeke" Modarelli and reprinted with her permission.

"Kindred," "Over Carson Valley," "Dawn—Washoe Valley," by Walter Van Tilburg Clark. "Kindred" first appeared in *Poetry*, copyright 1933 by the Modern Poetry Association and reprinted by permission of the editor of *Poetry*. "Dawn" from *Troubadour*, 1933. Reprinted by permission of the Walter Van Tilburg Clark Literary Estate.

"The Meeting Hour," by Elizabeth Perry. Copyright 1990 and reprinted with her permission.

"To a Dead Sailor of the Pacific," "Eastgate," "To Poets Unlimited," "The Shark," by Warren d'Azevedo. "To a Dead Sailor of the Pacific" from *Paper Pudding*, copyright 1973. "To Poets Unlimited" from *Brushfire*, copyright 1966, and reprinted by permission of Warren d'Azevedo.

"If You Should Die," "Hearing the Voices," "And One Other Thing," "For Montgomery Clift," "For a Lady Poet Gone Bureaucrat," "Vegas: A Few Scruples," "The Night Sammy Davis, Jr. Couldn't Go On (Las Vegas)," "The World Is Going to End Up in Burma," by A. Wilber Stevens. From *The World Is Going to End Up in Burma*. Copyright 1988 by A. Wilber Stevens. Reprinted by permission of Hardwood Books.

"Bottle," "Nursing Home," "My Father," "The Doctor Said," "Becoming Crippled," "Transcend," from *The Glass Hammer*. "Letters to Dare,"

"Meeting an Eel," "Jellyfish," "Hermaphroditus," "Talking to Zeus," from *Warm-Bloods, Cold-Bloods*. "Entering," "Late Letter to Walter Clark," "Old," "Three Meetings," "Stop," "Radiation," from *The Schoolhouse Poems*. Copyright 1983, 1981, 1975. Reprinted by permission of William L. Fox, executor of the literary estate of Joanne de Longchamps.

"American Lit, Interim," "Donner," "Vivaldi in Nevada," "Pyramid," "American Lit, The Ox-Bow Incident," "In Memory of Joanne de Longchamps 1923–1983, 1. Not Quite Yet," "The Oldest House in Silver City, Nevada," "Light on the Subject at Lehman Caves," by Harold Witt. From *Surprised by Others at Fort Cronkhite*, copyright 1975 by Sparrow Press; *The Death of Venus*, copyright 1958 by Harold Witt; "Pyramid" from *Beasts in Clothes*, copyright 1960, 1961, by Harold Witt and reprinted with permission of Macmillan Publishing Company; *Bristlecone*, copyright 1989 by Harold Witt; *Now, Swim*, copyright 1974 by Harold Witt; *The New York Times*, copyright 1967 by *The New York Times*; *Interim*, copyright 1989; *Piedmont Literary Review*, copyright 1988. Reprinted by permission of Harold Witt.

"Interlude," by Charles H. Crump. From *Brushfire*, copyright 1989. Reprinted by permission of Charles H. Crump.

"Cong Xin," "On Bats," "My Father's Martial Art," "I'm Entering Your Shadow," "A Sick Elephant," "In Disneyland," "Night on the Sea," "Homecoming for April," "On Qing Ming Festival," "How Abundant Is the Spring," "Redondo Beach," by Stephen Shu-Ning Liu. From *Dream Journeys to China*, copyright 1982 by New World Press. Reprinted by permission of Stephen Shu-Ning Liu.

"A Minor Carver," by William Abrams. From *West Coast Poetry Review*, copyright 1972. Reprinted by permission of William Abrams.

"A Parallel Cut of Air," "Travel, Tea, Home," "Each Takes One Leaf," "In His Compartment," by Elaine Dallman. From *A Parallel Cut of Air*, copyright 1990 by Elaine Dallman and reprinted with her permission.

"Let Me Know How You Feel," "After the Tornado," "The Helicopter," by James Hazen. From the *Painted Bride Quarterly*, copyright 1989; *The Galley Sail Review*, copyright 1988; and *The Cape Rock*, copyright 1989. Reprinted by permission of James Hazen.

"My Angel Contemplates Sin," "Why We Should Make Love in the Streets," "Always," "Memory Is a Thin Pine, Maybe Fir," by Dennis Parks. Reprinted by permission of Dennis Parks.

"Villanelle," by Peter Parsons. From *Interim*, copyright 1990 by Peter Parsons and reprinted with his permission.

"another cop-killing," "Saturday Rat Shoot and River Walk," "A Lesson in Plowing," by Ronald W. Manning. Reprinted by permission of Ronald W. Manning.

"12," "13," "11," "Maria Vladimirovna Lvov 1917–1941," "33, New York, Easter, 1983," by Tom Meschery. Reprinted by permission of Tom Meschery.

"Growing Up With the Drunks on Highway 66," "The Mormons," "From Casper to Cheyenne," "Texas Daddy," "Summer Colored Girl," "All Day Week Days," "Good-bye to My Cowboy Uncle," "Failure," by John Garmon. From *Mornings After the Nativity*, copyright by John Garmon 1976, *Llano Sons: Trips and Passings*, copyright 1989 by John Garmon, and *Quartet*. Reprinted by permission of John Garmon.

"Old Woman in Cold," by Elizabeth I. Riseden. Reprinted by permission of Elizabeth I. Riseden.

"Weight Watchers," by Robert Dodge. Reprinted with permission by Robert Dodge.

"Drifting," "Meeting Gandhi on the Markleeville Road," "Through Long Windows," "Steam Bellies and Cheap Coin," "Stillwater Refuge," by Bill Cowee. "Drifting" and "Through Long Windows" from *Comstock Chronicle*, copyright 1988; "Meeting Gandhi on the Markleeville Road" from *Interim*, copyright 1987; "Steam Bellies and Cheap Coin" from *Comstock Quarterly*, copyright 1989.

"Hypothermia," "Morning Glory," "Keyhole Canyon, Nevada," "Sacred Datura," "The Smokers," "Brandon," "Teacher," "Wednesday, November 16, 1988, 11:45 A.M.," by Joan Cutuly. "Keyhole Canyon, Nevada" from *Bristlecone*, copyright 1988. Reprinted by permission of Joan Cutuly.

"Handgrip," "Decay," "Whorehouse," "Primer," "Homing," "Homestead," "Kinship," "Suppers," by Billie Jean James. "Handgrip," and "Decay" from the *Nevadan Today*; "Whorehouse" from *San Marcos Review*; "Primer" from *Pulp: Fiction and Poetry*; "Homing" from *Southwest: A Contemporary Anthology*. Copyright 1990 by Billie Jean James and reprinted with her permission.

"Royal Copenhagen Plates," "Chastised," by Ursula Carlson. From *Brushfire*, copyright 1980. Reprinted by permission of Ursula Carlson.

"And Once I Was Irish, At Least," "A Lunist and His Lunism," "Sing,

Columnar Muse, of Me the Last in This Bin," by Thomas Whitehead. From *Bristlecone*, copyright 1988; *Beloit Poetry Journal*, copyright 1987; *Interim*, copyright 1987. Reprinted by permission of Thomas Whitehead.

"Getting in the Wood," "For Aunt Lizzie," "On the Edge," "The Wedge," by William Wilborn. "For Aunt Lizzie," "On the Edge," and "The Wedge" from *Rooms*, copyright 1990 by Cummington Press. Reprinted by permission of Cummington Press.

"This Town Sure Takes the Rattlebox," "They Buried Sonny Liston at the End of McCarran Airport Runway in Las Vegas," "On the Edge of Equilibrium," by Red Shuttleworth. "This Town Sure Takes the Rattlebox" and "They Buried Sonny Liston at the End of McCarran Airport Runway in Las Vegas" from *Calapooya Collage*. "On the Edge of Equilibrium," from *Western Movie*. Copyright 1990 by Red Shuttleworth and reprinted with his permission.

"The Car Hums," by Timothy Bellows. Reprinted by permission of Timothy Bellows.

"The Serenade of the Looking Glass," "Choices," "The Real Tragedy," "The Beating," "Another Santa Ana," by Bobbi Curry-Cartwright. Reprinted by permission of Bobbi Curry-Cartwright.

"The Warehouse Chronicle," "Fallon Rodeo Long Time Ago," "Epiphany: Oxymoron," "The Chicken Blues," "Indian Cemetery: Lovelock, Nevada," "Near Eighteenth Street," "Something About Being an Indian," "The First of the Month," by Adrian C. Louis. From *Fire Water World*, copyright 1989 by West End Press. Reprinted by permission of West End Press.

"Driving to Vegas," "Hopper," "Schwitters," "Outside Ely in the Rain," "Four or Five Beers," "All Day Long," "Adjusting to the Desert," "Not Quite Dark," "Drawing to an Inside Straight," by Kirk Robertson. From *Driving to Vegas, New and Selected Poems 1969–87*, copyright 1989 by SUN/gemini Press. Reprinted by permission of SUN/gemini Press.

"Desert Wind," "Antelope Rising," by Jean Boudreau. "Antelope Rising" from *Quicksilver*, copyright 1989 by Jean Boudreau. Reprinted by permission of Jean Boudreau.

"Despair I," "Our Brothers," "Waiting," "Back Pockets," by Milly Brown. Reprinted by permission of Milly Brown.

"The Side Effects of Hope-to-Die Brothers," by Jimi Sheryl Bufkin.

From *Sometimes My Mind Wanders and Wonders*, copyright 1988 by Jimi Sheryl Bufkin and reprinted with her permission.

"Plea," "A New View," "Cemetery at Virginia City," "The Healer," "On Entering My Fortieth Year," "On Frogs," "A Desperate Theory on the Meaning of Life," "Sea Story," "The Effects of Therapy on a Mad Mother," by Judy Carlisle. "Cemetery at Virginia City" from the *Comstock Chronicle*, copyright 1988; "A Desperate Theory on the Meaning of Life," "Sea Story," and "The Effects of Therapy on a Mad Mother" from *Brushfire*, copyright 1983. Reprinted by permission of Judy Carlisle.

"Lines," "Your Mother Taught You How to Fish," "Grandmother," "Steel," "Saturday Morning," "From the White Single Woman Middle Class Recession Blues: An Invention in Parts," "Remembering John," "Anniversary Poem: Weeds," "The Trout That Do Not Bite," by Melanie Perish. "Lines" from *Utah Holiday*, copyright 1984; "Your Mother Taught You How to Fish" from *Calyx*, copyright 1982; "Steel" from *13th Moon*, copyright 1983; "Saturday Morning" from *Notes of a Daughter from the Old Country*, copyright 1978; "Remembering John" from *Arulo*, copyright 1982.

"Kathmandu," "poem," "Rai Family," "Yarsa," "Dudh Kosi," "Chaurikharka," "Kanetega," "Thyangboche," "Breitenbach," "Lobuje (16,000 feet)," "Sherpa Woman," by William L. Fox. "Kathmandu," "Rai Family," "Yarsa," "Dudh Kosi," "Chaurikharka," "Kanetega," "Thyangboche," "Breitenbach," "Lobuje (16,000 feet)," and "Sherpa Woman" from *Time by Distance*, copyright 1985 by Duck Down Press; "poem" from *Iron Wind*, copyright 1971 by Sono Nis Press.

"The House on Buena Vista," "For Howard Nemerov, Summer 1979," "When the Vein Runs Out," "Waiting for Tomorrow," "Building the Pumphouse," by Jim Huskey. "For Howard Nemerov, Summer 1979" and "The House on Buena Vista" from *Portfolio I: Poems*, copyright 1979 by Sand Mountain Press; "Building the Pumphouse" from *Beacon Review*, copyright 1984 by *Beacon Review*. Reprinted by permission.

"Assent," by Robert McGinty. Reprinted by permission of Robert McGinty.

"Decidía no morirme," "Ya no se oye en la muerte," "Me había acostumbrado," "Esa muerte," "Aquí estoy yo ahora," "11 de septiembre de 1973," "El último rezo de septiembre," by Emma

Sepúlveda-Pulvirenti. "Decidía no morirme," "Ya no se oye en la muerte," and "Esa muerte" from *A la muerte y otras dudas*, copyright 1989; "Aquí estoy yo ahora," "11 de septiembre de 1973," and "El último rezo de septiembre" from *Tiempo cómplice del tiempo*, copyright 1990. Reprinted by permission of Ediciones Torremozas.

"Little red riding hood," "the way & the way things are," "warehouse poem," by nila northSun. "Little red riding hood" and "the way & the way things are" from *Diet Pepsi & Nacho Cheese*, copyright 1977 by Duck Down Press. Reprinted by permission of Duck Down Press and nila northSun.

"Requiem," "Now Her Small Grave," "Not Far From Our Town," "Lists That Follow," by Robin Elizabeth Davis. "Requiem" from the *Comstock Chronicle*, copyright 1988. Reprinted by permission of Robin Elizabeth Davis.

"A Place of Stone," by Shaun T. Griffin. From *The Redneck Review of Literature*, copyright 1988 by Shaun T. Griffin and reprinted by permission of the author.

"Toward Morning (Panaca, Nevada)," "Near Mina," "Farnes Egbert: Water Dowser," "Test," "John W. Mackay," "Two Poems About Wells, Nevada," "The Cave Behind the Mormon Church in Panaca," and "If the Kennecott Smelter in McGill Closes," by Gary Short. "Toward Morning (Panaca, Nevada)," from *Midwest Quarterly*, Summer 1990; "If the Kennecott Smelter in McGill Closes," from *Southwest American Literature*; "The Cave Behind the Mormon Church in Panaca," from *5 AM*, Volume 3, Summer 1990; "Near Mina," "Farnes Egbert: Water Dowser," "Test," "John W. Mackay," "Two Poems About Wells, Nevada," from *Looking Past Today*, copyright 1983 by Duck Down Press. Reprinted by permission of Duck Down Press and Gary Short.

"Final Recollections," by Roger Smith. From *Brushfire*, copyright 1980 by Roger Smith and reprinted by permission of the author.

"Out Walking," "Letter to an Absent Lover," "With Respect for Distance," "Neighbors," "The Swing," by Gailmarie Pahmeier. From *With Respect for Distance*, copyright 1990 by Gailmarie Pahmeier.

"Independence," "The Stepfather," "Fishing Lesson," by Kelly Moon. Reprinted by permission of Kelly Moon.

"The Rubdown," "Map," "Musing on Flower Poems," by L. A. Fleming. From *River City Magazine*. Copyright 1989 by L. A. Fleming and reprinted with her permission.

The editor would like to acknowledge receipt of a grant for editorial assistance from the Nevada State Council on the Arts, a state agency, in 1989.

Finally, I am deeply indebted to at least two people, without whom the book would have surely suffered—A. Wilber Stevens and Robert E. Blesse—dear friends both and careful eyes and ears for an editor ever in need of suggestion.

Thelma "Brownie" Ireland (1899–   )

Along with Irene Bruce and others, Thelma Ireland was a member of the Reno Poetry Workshop during the 1940s and has been a lifelong champion of poets and poetry in northern Nevada. Her work has appeared in many publications, including *Arizona Highways*, *Incredible Idaho*, *Ladies' Home Journal*, and several anthologies. She is an active member of the Reno Poetry Society and has been a great help to biographers, not unlike the editor of this volume, who are trying to piece together the literary pasts of many talented writers with whom Ireland has written and published throughout her long life.

HAIKU

The distant palm trees
Holding up the flaming sky
Momentarily.

AUTUMN OAK

Her stout arms akimbo
Through which the wind swirls,
The oak tree stands coiffured
With dried leaf brown curls.
The fall breeze brings warning.
She heeds not the words
For she's cloaked in sunshine
And buttoned with birds.

Irene Bruce (1903–1987)

Born in Texas, Irene Bruce moved to Nevada in 1936. In the 1940s she founded the Reno Poetry Workshop, conducted a poetry program on KOH radio, and was poetry editor for *Nevada Magazine*. During the 1950s she lived in Virginia City along with Walter Van Tilburg Clark and several other writers. Her poetry has appeared in numerous magazines, including the *Christian Science Monitor* and *New Mexico Quarterly*.

Sonnets for Harry. Reno, Nevada: Privately published, 1976.

Night Cry. Reno, Nevada: Poetry West, 1950.

Crag and Sand. Reno, Nevada: Silver State Press, 1945.

VIRGINIA CITY, NEVADA

The contrived glamor of tourists
glitters palely into this sudden village,
finding dregs of history scattered obscurely
over the rim of a high mountain canyon.
The travelers shiver as the sun stares at them bleakly,
and the tip of the wind catches their garments.

Images here are seldom seen
through pity-taunting eyes of tourists;—
for while they dip lightly into quarter history,
jerking at handles of coin-famished machines,
the embers of dust are stirring
the deeds of men whose deaths
laugh at their modern gestures.

SEA ROSE

We plucked a green sea rose
And held it against our lips,
Until the sifted pollen
Flowed to our fingertips.

And then we dipped our hands
Into a foaming sea,
And let the cooling sands
Prolong our ecstasy.

And when you felt we knew
Enough of sand and rose,
You drew my breath into
An ocean of repose.

RATTLESNAKE

Beware, but understand the rattlesnake:
He concentrates his craving of a fowl,
Which had to go in whole or not at all.
Two fangs, with which he strikes, can overtake
The startled beat of helpless hearts of prey.
He has no legs, and everywhere he goes
He crawls, uncoiled; his belly stalks his foes,
And outruns death for yet another day.
His rattle freezes unseen terror where
The tangled grasses subtly change their hue;
His fear is far beyond the fear in you:
He bites because your foot has pressed him there.

ARROWHEAD

Your flight now cold, you lie within a frame
Above a mantle, where the glance of years
Records your pageantry in place. One hears
Beyond the prisms of a hearth-warmed flame,
Beyond historic volumes flush with shame:
Hard hands that sharpened you into their fears
Once painted grimaces above their tears,
And lost their courage in a savage name.

Today you speak a specimen of time,
And fear-swift deer no longer leap from you;
Your feathers in the wind no longer mean
The hunter's hidden track, or warrior's crime,
Your agony and water-moon canoe
Are stoic shadows that are never seen.

Helen "Zeke" Modarelli (1905–1990)

A native of Salt Lake City, Utah, "Zeke" Modarelli received her B.S. from the University of Utah in 1927. On December 1, 1943—at the height of World War II—she moved to Elko, Nevada, to teach in a one-room school at a mining camp outside of town. There her husband was seriously injured and his brother died in a mining accident, but she continued to teach and was a correspondent for the *Salt Lake Tribune*. For years she lived in northeastern Nevada (Elko, Wendover) before relocating to Carson City where she lived for over twenty years. She was an active member of the Ash Canyon Poets, and she wrote and rewrote her poems as if she had just begun. As she approached her mid-eighties, poetry did much to keep her alive. Her work appeared in *The Meadows*, *The Truckee*, and others.

RESIGNATION

At the moment of awakening
        the guilt of my frailties,
                like the pointed finger
of the village gossip,
                                overwhelms me;
I think I am quietly going mad.

Walter Van Tilburg Clark (1909–1971)

Walter Clark was born outside East Orland, Maine. At the age of eight he came to Reno, where his father became president of the University of Nevada. Most of his poetry was written while in college, before he turned to fiction. After publishing his first volume of verse, *Ten Women in Gale's House*, he went on to become Nevada's most prominent fiction writer in the 1940s and 1950s. After teaching high school in New York State and Virginia City, he taught at the University of Nevada, Reno, the University of Montana, and San Francisco State College before returning to the University of Nevada. He is perhaps best remembered in a poem by Joanne de Longchamps, "Late Letter to Walter Clark." His epic poem *Strange Hunting*, which was the precursor to his novel *The Track of the Cat*, was published by Black Rock Press in 1985.

Editor of *The Journals of Alfred Doten, 1849–1903* (three volumes). Reno, Nevada: University of Nevada Press, 1973.

The Watchful Gods and Other Stories. New York, New York: Random House, 1950.

The Track of the Cat. New York, New York: Random House, 1949.

The City of Trembling Leaves. New York, New York: Random House, 1945.

The Ox-Bow Incident. New York, New York: Random House, 1940.

Ten Women in Gale's House (poems). Boston, Massachusetts: Christopher, 1932.

KINDRED

This is not today's pain that is in me,
This ache of dying autumn in the drum of my chest,
This longing in the marrow tubes of my hidden bones,
This crying that watches the blackbirds flurry and eddy, full of intention,
That sees the armor of frost on the pale grass at dawn
And hears the mountain streams in bells of ice
Going down through the fire-storm of trees turned and now passing.
Somewhere out of my searching eyes the stronger predecessor looks

From a high rock ledge. With this pain in his sky-turned face,
With the cold wind steadily blowing the hair of his shoulders
He watches the arrowhead of the wild swan shooting south,
Diminishing under the low bed of the clouds;
And gropingly seeking the ease of his tangled strength,
He also moves among the crags, in the continual overpassing of birds
Down from the northern edge of summer.
I, remaining under the chatter of leaves, must die with the year.

OVER CARSON VALLEY

Heavy, and stolid, and blotting the high dark,
The vast soul of Dat-so-la-lee*
Squats cross legged upon the peaks,
Interlacing moon lances with wrinkled fingers,
Setting the warp and woof with stars,
Weaving a basket of space
To hold the cool of unlimited night
And pour it down over the desert at dawn.

DAWN—WASHOE VALLEY

Slowly the world tips,
The new sun spills
Over the edge
Down the blue eastern hills.
The poplar fingers stretch
Long, cool shadows toward
The white, light-struck Sierras
Up pressing the west sky,
All about the valley,
The copper-throated barn-yard muezzins cry:
"Dawn! Dawn! New dawn is here!"

*Editor's note: Dat-so-la-lee was a Washoe Indian who wove over one hundred remarkable baskets at the turn of the century.

Elizabeth Perry (1918–   )

A native of Manhattan, New York, Elizabeth Perry received her M.A. in languages and literature from Columbia University. For fourteen years she taught Spanish and English at Cathedral Preparatory School in Manhattan before moving to southern Nevada in 1982. The founding editor of *Pegasus* (1986), she now publishes the quarterly in Boulder City, a small community on the Colorado River south of Las Vegas. Her poetry has been published in *Interim*, *Midwest Poetry Review*, *Parnassus*, *Orphic Lute*, and other publications. A multilingual poet, she recently completed *Olé, Olé*, a series of poems about Spain. She makes her home at the foot of the River and McCullough ranges, five miles away from Hoover Dam.

Olé, Olé. Boulder City, Nevada: Pegasus Publishing, 1990.

THE MEETING HOUR

Before Dawn
drops
her luminous
petals
I wake
and listen
for your muted voice
to break the silence
of our worlds
like rustlings
in the deep woods.
It is our moment
shared
between black
and white hours
repeating pledges
like children

where neither
guilt
nor groundless fears
intrude
before you tighten
your somber robe
and I turn
ready for
the blameless light.

Warren d'Azevedo (1920–   )

Born in Oakland, California, Warren d'Azevedo was a merchant seaman during World War II. He returned to study at Berkeley and later to Northwestern, where he earned his Ph.D. in anthropology. He spent the majority of his teaching career at the University of Nevada, Reno, from which he recently retired. His African and North American ethnology studies have been widely published. His book on the Washoe Peyote religion is a large, hand-printed edition with woodcut illustrations and is now a collector's item. His poems have appeared in *California Quarterly*, *Paper Pudding*, and other publications.

Straight with the Medicine: Washoe Peyotist Narratives. Reno, Nevada: Black Rock Press, 1978.

The Traditional Artist in African Societies. Bloomington, Indiana: Indiana University Press, 1973.

The Gola of Liberia. New Haven, Connecticut: HAR-Flex Books, 1972.

TO A DEAD SAILOR OF THE PACIFIC

(On first seeing the Sailors' Union
memorial bust to Harry Lundberg.)

So Harry, it has come to this has it?
Your Swede's eye, round as grommet holes, once scanned
beaches like a seagull's. Now you're corked,
deep six in a lubber's grave, at that, and stowed
with proper shore against the genteel sod.
Stumpfarm dirt will stain, in time, the stiff
white cap and Frisco jeans. O Harry! Listen!
Can you hear the wild goons trampling up
on Rincon Hill? It's Maxie's finny ghost
who herds them from fogged alleys at the Front.
They put your bronzed head 'longside Andy's there,
to grace the marble Hall you built with deals:

But all the dumped gazoonies passing by
look sharp, and wink a shrewd dispassioned eye.

EASTGATE

the green feathered cock
crowed and split the night
from sagebrush fence flapped
a wing and pecked glazed tail
quills perched on one yellow
foot clenched in the halfstrut
of fowls listening to far-off
dogs bark
                    heard a truck
whine through the salt flat up
Frenchman's Grade shifting gears
its black shape square against
the edge of sky and thunder
cloud lumined by cold burning
stars careening past the red
constellation of running lights

TO POETS UNLIMITED

For William Carlos Williams

Poets are so
numerous we are
up to our bungs in worlds
unlived; yet

I have read
Williams
now and then. I
like the fact

he was a doc-
tor, an enemy
of death, and therefore
would not gamble.

He got down
to cases—never primped
or showed his ass
to just anyone.

What counted
with him was
the lone mind's speech.
He wrote it

as a measure
of health, a surgery
by language, a tonic of
ordinary things: and

this is to know
what art is—more a way
of doing than what's
done or praised.

THE SHARK

Wrapping his blanket round
he climbed down
off the rented bed
begging them to take him
to that place he knew
by the sea where
he slept on the sand once
with someone loved

They took him there
grieving yet sure
it was the thing to do and
not believing signs
left him there
thinking to return early
in the morning

Sitting on the ledge he
watched them go
before he took the painful steps
into the surf
saw some sea bats and stumbled
through the tangled kelp
began to swim and soon
lay back to float and felt
the cold hard swell of waves
sweep him out to dark sky
the swirl of stars and
stinging spray

He turned to cry once
for help and
seeing no one
feeling no expected revelation
only bitter crest of sea
called for shark
and shark came.

A. Wilber Stevens (1921–)

Born in Brooklyn, New York, and raised in Manhattan, A. Wilber Stevens received his Ph.D. in English from the University of Washington. While attending there, he studied with Richard Hugo, Theodore Roethke, and Carolyn Kizer. He founded *Interim* in 1944, which he edited for the following ten years. With time out for Fulbright-sponsored trips to Thailand and Burma, he spent the next several years as a dean or faculty member at universities in the West. When he moved to Nevada in 1973, he resurrected the literary magazine at the University of Nevada, Las Vegas, where he is currently a professor of English. His poems have appeared in numerous publications, among them *New Mexico Humanities Review*, *Poetry Northwest*, *The Literary Review*, and *Smoky Hill Review*. Along with a core of other southern-Nevada poets, he has done much to shape the poetry of that region in the 1970s and 1980s.

Co-Editor, *Indian Poetry in English*. Calcutta, India: Writers' Workshop, 1989.

The World Is Going to End Up in Burma. Carson City, Nevada: Hardwood Books, 1988.

Stories Southwest. Prescott, Arizona: Prescott College Press, 1970.

Poems Southwest. Prescott, Arizona: Prescott College Press, 1968.

IF YOU SHOULD DIE

If you should die in my house
I will be afraid of the wind which brought you
When they take you down the stairs evenly
And deposit you like cotton in the car
And then take you down again to take your blood
I will know my house is not right for me.

I cannot bring you back again
And if this banal truth is true you should not die
You should not die at least in my home
Where there is a speaking tube and an old piano
And where people once sang at evenings
And where my father lay dead to receive my child kiss.

If you should die in my house
And if there were an ocean near my window lights
I would crawl on my roof and fly over the strapped thing
They use to take people like you to lower rooms
Those tax free rooms full of silence and sirens and coffee
Where already I lie dead with you cold and stone and true.

HEARING THE VOICES

The cheap drum set presides
Over his abandoned scattered room
The visible inventory stammers
Like a threat to his keening solitude.

On the gaping desk rejected books
Except for Sidney Omar on Aquarius
A green model spitfire made in "there"
And brought home on pass
For one infested try at freedom
The Mad Scientists Affair
The other honored book under disgorged
Tape decks a glasses case (the glasses
Crushed he never wore them) a dead Palm
Saved from an unblessed Sunday
His own initialled pewter cup
Full of black spit he still asks
For gifts of Copenhagen to chew
While he listens for "them" three
Pictures of the one named Kitty dark

And musing found with him in the Phoenix
Bus station the Stones upon the cork walls
His dead mother's picture by the stereo
Two dumbbells a scrawled letter to himself
Titled "My Future Focus" two tennis rackets
Under AC/DC McEnroe over the bed Gerulaitis
Covering the hole his head made in the door.

Today he is sixteen
I strike the cymbal
He is gone
He has taken the voices with him.

AND ONE OTHER THING

I should have died a Trojan or a Spartan
Or someone mechanical or full of deadly machines
I keep seeing the more morbid side of things
When you get right down to it really
I should have been a headwaiter or a good lover
Or a Chairman preferably of someone else's Board
I keep wondering—perhaps a quiet doctor
Charging a lot and never saying much.

I should have died Established or at least Taboo
Instead I leave my card and shun the Out-Of-Doors
And wonder why I should have died not being
That very Thing I should have been whether
Secluded in some New Hampshire village waging
Wisdom or perhaps wondering bitter things
Oh so sullen Things in a desert some place where
I could have died complete and whole and all alone.

FOR MONTGOMERY CLIFT

One night it was a raining Tuesday
I saw him young in Providence
In a bad bird-eye play about freedom.
My sense was then and is now
That he knew more about the play
Than the play did and that his special
Haunting of the stage came with
Coffee, some sea and our distant fears.

FOR A LADY POET GONE BUREAUCRAT

Sundry female poet friend you noisy one
God I love to see you wear that blazer hear that blast
I feel the luncheon look and knowing smiling when
We are at table together in the hinters and haunters
I love you constantly though on the run I cannot
Find you in the motel nor by the pool I keep
Finding your files everywhere and want to bring
Them to you but people keep saying that you have
Already left for Syracuse to address a rally or
Spring some poor assistant professor who cruised
And picked up fuzz by mistake and almost lost
His Guggenheim really honey I have a poem I want
You to hear not the one you said was "putrid" in La Grande
Nor the one you said was "too titty" in El Paso
I mean the one about us when the houseboat almost sank
And you decided then and there that you would never
Laugh again and the water around us seemed to die
And we went away and came upon all these our foolish ways.

VEGAS: A FEW SCRUPLES

Under scrutiny of hills in the hot sun
A woman crazed has cut her lover
Hacked at his privacies kicked
Glass at him broken glass is the thing
Here where the children at the lower
Elementary levels have one of the best
Systems and more daysleeping parents
Than Monaco it's a tight town
Full of churches rampant cars like
Pimples mapping the alleys behind
The Strip a wonderment of sullen searchers
Planted firmly on the shifty earth looking.

When Brigham sent his band here
He did not foresee what the sun could
Do but burn for the Faith it does burn
Indeed burn right for the Saved of which
There are many species transient and nested
And too there are the lesser breeds the maniac
The levitated professors who floated
Into this crude escrow like bad seeds vagrant
Talent dumped from the more thoughtful cities
All sorts of burning bushes in dry tide
Now by gardens and pools the natives half watch
The cuffed change girl shuffle to the cool blue car.

THE NIGHT SAMMY DAVIS, JR. COULDN'T GO ON (LAS VEGAS)

I am still astonished
Years ago he danced with his uncle
And with his father in Seattle
He imitated Cary Grant
The world ran through him

He jumped on sixteen feet
Played the flute with his toes
Then I read that he wouldn't open
This time in Las Vegas the strike was on
The music was cold
Sammy had to sit things out
The night couldn't wake up
The bones were willing
But no tone poems to play with
Sammy couldn't run walk or sing
Oh how still a room can get
When the cats are quiet.

THE WORLD IS GOING TO END UP IN BURMA

The world is going to end up in Burma
There with the water buffalo and the roads
The sun as hot as history
The northern rains the quakes the blessed people
Worshippers there is where it will all end
In Burma with its trembling people their
Longyis sopping with monsoon their purses
Empty from monks and Chinese and every
God talking to them about the way the way
Oh it will end in Burma I promise you that
All the teak beds will moan not with love
But with crackling of the walls of the compounds
With final chorus the students will weep with rage
Be lost and the rice will die and all those outside
Coming in will join with the end of the world
In Burma where the gold leaf and the queens
And the old empire joined and died and died.

Joanne de Longchamps (1923–1983)

From the 1950s to the late 1970s, Joanne de Longchamps was one of the most widely respected poets to emerge from this state. A native of Los Angeles, she was active in the Reno Poetry Workshop in the 1940s and worked closely with Harold Witt, Irene Bruce, and Thelma "Brownie" Ireland to form the nucleus of a thriving literary community in Reno. Many things made Joanne special, among them her collages, inspired by Greek mythology, and her later poem/collage combinations. As with all lasting art, her poem/collages stretched its boundaries and as a result we are left with a legacy of artistic triumph despite her lifelong battle with multiple sclerosis and the suicide of her only son Dare. Though she published numerous books, and poems in the *New York Times*, *New Mexico Magazine*, and *Southwest Review*, she remained virtually unknown outside of the state. To all who knew her, this was a terrible contradiction, but one that is slowly changing. She was the first Walter Van Tilburg Clark lecturer in creative writing at the University of Nevada, Reno, and like him, showed us Nevada through the eyes of a stunningly gifted artist.

The Glass Hammer (posthumous manuscript). Reno, Nevada: The literary estate of Joanne de Longchamps, William L. Fox, executor, 1983.

Warm-Bloods, Cold-Bloods (poems and collages). Reno, Nevada: West Coast Poetry Review Press, 1981.

One Creature (poems and collages). Reno, Nevada: West Coast Poetry Review Press, 1977.

The Schoolhouse Poems. Reno, Nevada: West Coast Poetry Review Press, 1975.

The Wishing Animal. Nashville, Tennessee: Vanderbilt University Press, 1970.

The Hungry Lions. Bloomington, Indiana: Indiana University Press, 1963.

Eden Under Glass. Francetown, New Hampshire: Golden Quill Press, 1957.

And Ever Venus. West Los Angeles, California: Wagon and Star Publications, 1944.

BOTTLE

I have banished you, playmate,
after hundreds of partings,
rushes of reconciliation.
I have stoppered your mouth
and my babbling.
I say no to the overcast
days you drape over me.
And I miss you,
your firm shape,
your sweet juices,
our nights locked together.

We were consumed
without dalliance or fore-play.
All, all went down with us
to the dark kingdoms,
to craved unconsciousness—
from ardor to stupor,
safe from the rub of dreams.

You wait for me in a thousand rooms.
You travel on trains and ships,
all glassy sparkle, a party-boy
at zero latitude
toasting the future.

Now I say no.
Now I dread and dream
the moment of our next embrace—
tipped up and tupping face to face.

NURSING HOME

I'm tired of trying to find warm girls
who lived and lay down
inside these fierce old women—

exhausted, straining to see
lively ambitious girls
now curled here, sodden in half-sleep.

I'm stilled, pierced at heart
by youth, bonfires and sparklers
flaring in ancient eyes.

MY FATHER

called me Gold-Digger.
My God, that kid'll
nickel me to death, he said.
He was a warm bear, my father—
hair sprouted from his shoulders.
How his look hated me Sunday mornings,
waking him, slithering down
in the grand big bed,
parting him from my silken mother.

I was safe in the family hollow—
my first snug cave.

THE DOCTOR SAID:

Describe your pain.

I was silent.
Last night in rain I rode
to the river-road, saw the snowmelt
waters twist in flood.

What color is your pain,
what shape, what size?
It is silt and dung-brown.
It drags me under,
tosses me with ripped branches,
with entire trees whose roots
make frantic gestures in the cold.

Doctor, I am a turtle
with frozen feet,
locked in a shell of stone,
hurtled and tumbled—not yet
cracked open on river rock.

TRANSCEND,

that *word:*
legs twist useless, it commands me
to walk in beauty, house a host
of flawless dancers in my head,
fabricate a world of wonders.

If fingers can contort to claws,
the truth is rage and grief,
not miraculous transcendence.

I shall not paint a picture
with a brush held in my teeth.

BECOMING CRIPPLED

The time comes. I feel
earth fall, failing me
with no footholds, toe and heel
betrayed by slippery grass,
by stones forbidding trespass—
Of course it is I who am falling.

I feel it come, pressing near,
pillow and chair-time.
It is almost here
beyond all courage or act
but a matter of fact—
so simple, a matter of failing.

I choose my masks,
opt for dry elegance,
a sedentary dance.
When these, and wry humor, fail
find me curled inward, still,
steel-trapped, a creature—waiting.

LETTERS TO DARE

Darling,
I have been written to
I have been visited by
I have been on the phone with
women whose sons were suicides,
women making it through
the spike-lined knothole
the ice-hung night caves
the black earthdreams—

. . .

I write to you with a yellow pencil
lettered in brown: *No. 2.5*
Western Michigan University.
The eraser is almost gone.

Night into day, Kalamazoo to Reno,
telephone wires stretched umbilical—
but words could not nourish you.
No doors in your mind, no exits.
Even as you called, the walls closed in,
the lines went down. Then you came home.

. . .

My son with the brave name,
you dared to die.
How careful you were.
How neatly you taped your car windows,
fixed the hose to the motor—
(and you were the one who said
I'm not clever with my hands.)
In the glove compartment a young detective found
the receipt for rubber tubing
dated four days before—
days you had slept and risen,
bathed and smiled, seen friends,
listened to my latest poem
and for the first and last time
polished your grandmother's silver.

I could think:
now he feels better.
I could cook,
we could exclaim at mealtimes.
A leg-of-lamb feast—
last supper.

You offered help with the dishes.
You said: *I'm going to see a friend.*
Did you kiss me that leaving?
I don't remember.
I hear: *I'll see you later*
and keep the sight of your long,
long pausing at our door
opening to the night.
Was your friend at home?

. . .

I thank your father
and I thank you
for that school-year,
that nine months course.
Not before, not since
have I known such comradeship.
Frog in my pool,
newt in my pond,
we formed each other.
We communicated in deep, watery ways.
During that term, learning you,
I was never lonely.
You hiccupped in my belly,
rib-stretcher, breath-binder—
I even think you laughed.
We were the best of good company.

I am not surprised
waking into barrenness
from dreams of pregnancy.

. . .

All things attach to you
who are so separate.
Running away from home
and "the presence of your absence,"
flying to the sea-torn tip of Baja,

soaring and sinking through cumuli,
you were there—your loss was there.
Now I gather photographs of skies
and paste them down.
This paper country of clouds,
this artifice, as near as I,
unbeliever, can lean toward heaven.

. . .

Your great-aunt said:
He is never ruffled.
Man of masks and false calm.
Vulnerable, tender, you moved among
lost children in locked wards.
In zero latitudes of night,
hunched over the phone
you listened to the abandoned, the sad—
and answered every crisis call except your own.

You watered the rats in the cages and mazes
of a basement lab in Michigan.

. . .

Even in remembering,
I change you.
For every word written
the opposite seems true.
You were my living weight
of contradiction—
dead, you are the same,
synonym and antonym.
No single image keeps or captures
you in my rooms of love,
my house of shifting mirrors.

. . .

Dare,
I still get letters
urging me to feel no guilt
for your going. I feel none.
You were generous,
our love was wide-open—
to my mind you were scrupulously fair
and your death hides no mother's moral.
You were simply, complicatedly,
a good fighter downed.
I like what Hellman said:
"Guilt is often an excuse for not thinking."
And these lines from Gregory's new poem:
"I have been a boy fist-fighting against old
Iron Jaw, Death. I lost."

. . .

Without you I live
in another country,
country of cold.
I am making a collage of frosty papers.
I am forming a snow-queen,
mistress of arctic wolves.
She is Beauty and Death and Pride—
Yes, she is your bride.

MEETING AN EEL

may be eerie but not dangerous
unless
you're a swimmer in the Orinoco
River
where numerous eels are electric.
"They produce an electrical shock
strong enough to knock down a horse

and which reaches a voltage of 500
and a wattage of 40 as proved
by experiments in aquaria."

Eels are elongate   sinuous
wallowers in languorous shallows
                              writhers
in sensuous inlets   rising
only to gulp for air.
When sex strikes they head for the sea.
"Spawning occurs in deep water."

The larvae of eels are named *elvers*.
The currents they ride are called *eelfares*.
Such lyrical nomenclature
links science to poems. Still
I keep wondering about
that shocking experiment   that
knocked-down horse.

JELLYFISH,

                    you are
a maypole floating blue ribbons
wound into love-knots,

a water-wind parachute dangling
a tangle of cords,

a fluted cup of clear gelatin
turned upside-down,

a pastel umbrella tree
fluttering downdrifts of vines.

You are a hanging garden
braiding the sea.

HERMAPHRODITUS

Two figures near a fountain,
a man who would escape—
and a determined woman.
The myth tolls with his beauty
and her lust. He, the spawn of gods,
she, a wanting water-nymph.
He dove, she followed—
and she captured him.
Their gods, admirers of action,
fused them in amorous mid-dive,
a clever two-in-one.

To read somewhere that marriage
is flawed androgyny—
To think of mergings, the disparate joined,
duality drowned, made solitary—
Imaging flight and capture,
the desperate shocking plunge,
hands that cling like sea-stars,
breath rising in bubble constellations—
Imagine this
then know a single thing, as true as water
that closes over a sinking stone:
toward their endings, old men,
old women, resemble one another.

TALKING TO ZEUS

I stumble over this one, Zeus,
Danaë locked in a cell
to keep her chaste
and you, great woman-chaser,
the clever contriver, slipping through
her slotted prison window

to ravish in a rain of gold—
sperm swimming down
in coins, thin as gold-leaf.

Of course, for poetry's sweet shape,
I should vision a godly visitation,
even ungodly rape—
but no subtlety of swan or cloud,
no bull bravura here
and I fumble this one, Zeus,
thinking of the old story,
spread legs for cold cash.

ENTERING

I would write here,
learn coyote by his laughter,
lizard by quick looking,
fix chipmunk chitter and birdcry.
On good days they enter a poem.
Each by its nature comes,
sounding or silent, to the pines
I place in my lines.

Words for wind-shelter, stove-warmth,
the cabin a landed ark
but night was terror and wildness
trapped in the chimney flue—
thumping, fighting my firelight.

Ashes of morning now, quiet.
I wait for creatures to come
where death, uninvited, enters a poem.

LATE LETTER TO WALTER CLARK

Marking the year's circle
in your absence,
I date this mid-November.
Here at timberline, the creek shallows
freeze in sharp nights, thaw toward noon.
Mount Rose has her first shawl of snow.
Just now "a hawk sailed up
out of the white mountain."
A year for hawks—
my year for watching them.
They cross your trembling valley
between two peaks; exalted Rose
and the humped black bulk of Peavine.

Those who met on a snowhill
for the opening and closing
of cold earth given you,
spoke of deep grayness—then
of stasis mercifully broken:
the sun rayed out in skyspace,
catching a sudden spiral
and wheeling wings granted
the healing movement of birds.

Invisibly, a great hawk soared
and scattered the starling flock:
"gaining height against the wind . . .
the light golden in the fringe of his plumage."

OLD

She waits for me,
an old woman
with bristles on her chin:

waits in a room
where the mirrors
mock dewlaps and doddering:

the flesh of her arms
sways out from the bone,
her feet are clumsy and numb:

her hands are stiff,
and twisted blue veins
snake under the skin.

. . .

I hope she is warm
in a comfort of cats
and fleece lap-robes;

and I wish her
a punctual visitor
who brings brandy and flowers.

She waits down-corridor,
that next to last door
I will enter.

THREE MEETINGS

1.

In the wheelchair line-up
we shared an ashtray
and waited for underground doors
to open on a black machine
where sharp green lightning
streaks a screen

as flesh-hooked needles
graph a brain.

2.

Upstairs, ward-walking,
we met again.
He was half my age,
broad as an Angus,
black-browed, beautiful.
I smiled. He spoke:
Grand Mal, three seizures,
four nurses knocked down—

Out of that well that waits maternal
I surfaced, stroked his shoulder.
I'm a farm boy, he told me.
I answered
You're a damn good-looking one
and a grin broke his frown.
You too, he offered, and we walked on.

3.

In the TV room
we shared an ashtray
and watched green wiggles on a screen.
Lousy set, he said. *Hey,*
let's shower together—
only way we'll find out.
When a blond nurse came
at bedtime hour,
I loosed the most lewd, non-maternal
wink in my repertoire
and the boy winked back. *Say,*
see you around.

But I left the next day.

STOP

A wise man wrote
that, given daily-ness, each one of us
should have a *howling room.*
Yes, that, and also
Time must have a stop—
but a stop within Time,
not an end, not death.
Even as avid lovers need
nights that endure for a year,
we, within our bodies and our time,
require a recess from that rigid school
teaching us each day that we must die.
I see that room: a bubble filled with flowers
where the self, encapsulated,
can loll, love, howl—or gorgeously
sleep away day's disciplines.
And while we are loving, sleeping,
no greedy clock-hands move, no one goes hungry
or needs us, no one sickens or dies.

Think how we should break beautifully
forth from that bubble reborn,
remade and ready for our bodies and our time.

RADIATION

Here the threshold guardian
is a cautious therapist.
He wears a lead apron.
He makes me walk through lead doors.
Mid-center in his basement room,
the altar bed is clean and cold—
white as a lamb in a night shirt,
I am arranged thereon

and over my heart a metal arm
swivels in and settles down.
So leap away and lock me in,
flip a switch and set the timer,
I am a six-minute egg
cooked daily for six weeks.
I am a slow burn.
I am afraid.

Under the cobalt cone
that stares with one white eye,
time does tricks with time
and now it is impossible
not to be unwilling Jonah
praying out of the fish's belly—
for three days and three nights only
after the sea encompassed him,
after salt-weeds bound in his head.
When Jonah came out of his vault,
did he have wide welts and skin-burns
from rubbing on the rib-bones,
from rushing through those teeth
in the whale's vomiting kiss?

Nowhere do they tell of this.

Harold Witt (1923–   )

Though Harold Witt has been away from Nevada for some time, this state and its poets have long held a central place in his poetry. He was close friends with Joanne de Longchamps and Irene Bruce, both of whom he first learned of during World War II while living in a camp for conscientious objectors at Galena Creek. Bruce and de Longchamps were co-editing *Destinies*, and after Witt sent them his poetry the three met in the Reno Poetry Workshop. He later was the reference librarian for Washoe County Library before eventually settling in Orinda, California. A founding editor of *Blue Unicorn*, he is the author of eleven books/chapbooks of poetry. His work has appeared in *The New Yorker*, *Saturday Review*, *Hudson Review*, *Poetry Northwest*, *The New Republic*, and others. He is the recipient of the James D. Phelan Award and the Emily Dickinson Award among others. For several years he has been working on a series of poems entitled *American Lit*, some of which appear here. Rereading the preface he wrote for Irene Bruce's book *Night Cry* in 1950, I am reminded that many good writers were working beneath "Twain's vast Nevada going rose / purple and mauve at dusk, as it still does."

The Snow Prince. Kensington, California: *Blue Unicorn*, 1982.

Surprised by Others at Fort Chronkhite. West Lafayette, Indiana: Sparrow Press, 1975.

Now, Swim. Ashland, Ohio: The Ashland Poetry Press, 1974.

Beasts in Clothes. New York, New York: Macmillan, 1961.

Winesburg by the Sea. Austin, Texas: Thorp Springs Press, 1979.

AMERICAN LIT
INTERIM

Someone at the Reno workshop read—
probably Joanne—a marvelous poem,
in a low, vibrant voice, tilting her head,
from a magazine called *Interim*:
"The Foetus," I recall—Wendell B. Anderson.

It was like an x-ray, glowing bones,
and veins that flowed with blood under the skin—
I'd never heard such vivid verbs and nouns,
only lately realized I'd floated
nine slow months in amniotic dark,
a person growing while my mother bloated,
before that, if it wasn't quite the stork
that brought me, I felt more like Shelley—
diaphanous-winged and never in a belly.

DONNER

Trapped at the top, when it seemed we couldn't get down—
two huge trucks stuck, blinking on roseate snow
where flares hissed and men danced in their boots to keep warm,
we stopped in a sleet cloud, the heater cooling to zero,
our steel a thin curved canvas flapping in pioneer storm.

The updated concrete highway, wide enough for summer,
frozen to winter surmise, bent rutted and narrow
into white flakes falling in a headlight shimmer.
The studded roadside signs were blotting dimmer and dimmer.
The bones of our pampering suddenly felt their marrow.

Our feet recalled ancestral veins and ankles
bitten and blaned, and a freeze too steep for wool
seeped through the glass, drifted up to the axles,
diminished on blankness figures that might look tall
shining in summer, but moved there helpless and small.

O snowburned pioneers, willing a way,
tugged by torn horses through that tortuous chill,
devouring the corpses of cold necessity—
Donner, Donner, we thought as they towed away
easy obstacles and we inched downhill.

VIVALDI IN NEVADA

Hear, while around the rodeo grounds below
a girl gallops her pale palomino
and like a cowboy film a man in Stetson
follows, incongruous, Vivaldi's *Concerto Grosso*.

The local colors flapped Reno Rodeo,
the parade, with clowns, passed serious and slow;
some succumbed to heat, some heaped the queen
with roses; sales went up on beer and beaded Coke.

They roped, and broke steers, and one was thrown
to twitch on crutches inglorious afternoons
but listen—listen to Vivaldi,
the dateless, deathless drama of his tones.

The West passed like a brief excitement,
like bands in red boomed in burnt down towns;
Vivaldi, while those who pranced in the purple mountains
lie under summer still as stones, plays on.

PYRAMID

The desert cries with gulls, the dry is wet—
in violence like this, disciples might
toss and toss until toward their boat
a raying savior walked through wests of light.
Then radiance of aftermath might lap
shores like these, pelicans resurrect
and, where swans slide too, farfetchedly flap
beaks, wings, webs, applauding their own éclat.

Beside weird shapes of tufa where they slept,
snakes might unwind and faintly castanet,
cui-uis leap through lavenders of quiet,
the purple pyramid turn to burning red—

Marvelous loaves, and water into wine,
infinities of fin where none had swum—
miracles as likely as this shine
and shadow-shattered coming of the night
to such a lake, a place where nature seems
—raying with changing ranges, windrow-lined—
symbolic splendor; suspending disbelief,
we walk the Christ-calmed mirrors of that deep.

AMERICAN LIT
THE OX-BOW INCIDENT

In God We Trust it said on every coin,
which I believed, and sang hymn after hymn;
there wasn't any mob that I would join
(though cheered a little for the jaycee team)
so if it came to choosing what to do,
kill or be killed, or if outnumbered, hang,
you'd see me either beaten black and blue
or strung up on a branch by some mad gang—
the West, by my time wasn't quite so wild
or so I thought, but why then was I nervous?
To every male who'd lately been a child
there came that notice from Selective Service—
the nation still a land without a law
except the early one, of tooth and claw.

IN MEMORY OF JOANNE DE LONGCHAMPS 1923–1983

1. Not Quite Yet

You phone to say, if not quite yet goodbye,
that what was done to you was done too late,
the stitches which they took were not in time
and nothing now is left except to die
though you don't know how long you'll have to wait—
and you may be resigned to death but I'm
unresigned to yours—and war and crime
and calling any morbid horror fate
and staying calm as you seem though you say
you have been drinking some and then you state—
I almost see the twinkle in your eye—
you're leaving me your color RCA
and then as on that first green Reno day
both of us laugh while trying not to cry.

THE OLDEST HOUSE IN SILVER CITY, NEVADA

Stone by stone, Irene's remade the mountain
to keep its natural erosions out of the house,
toting buckets of water to every sprig:
she's eked an Eden from the desert dryness—
a tree of heaven fans us with green shade.

Harry, dapperly capped, also looks proud
of what she's done, and tells about the lizard
coming to drink—laughs about the time
she guided a tarantula across the road,
talking to it as if it were a child.

"They're useful animals," Irene laughs at herself
"and we need all the helpers we can get."
With its new roof and newly gleaming sides,
you wouldn't guess the little house had stood
over a century among abandoned mines.

She picks a yellow brilliance from the hill
and tells the children it's a "Miner's Lantern."
Inside, we're shown a picture of the house,
shining as now, a stagecoach down below.
"People are always coming to take pictures."

And we take ours—Harry and Irene
smiling out from their front porch frontier—
from farther on we'd let the camera zoom
back through the miles of sage where year by year
houses and supermarkets spread like a poison mushroom.

LIGHT ON THE SUBJECT AT LEHMAN CAVES

Amazed in a maze, led on by a ranger
we went through stone curtains patience had dripped
to Xanadu rooms—chapel and chamber,
towers that tilted as centuries slipped,

corridor, archway, pale floor of flowing—
the dark pronged beneath and pooled for whom?—
light on the subject—the ranger was showing
stalactites below in a watery room—

a purpose revealed, in pallid perfection
sharp shapes upreaching, deep in the pool,
and from the roof, reaching down toward reflection
like splinters of light at the heart of a jewel.

He turned out the light, on an edge of our knowing,
as death does—and loveliness changed to a pit—
where we had come from and where we were going
arrested in blackness, negated by that,

but we laughed, and went on, the way we had come,
climbers on dimness, hiking toward what
we had left at the top—a sense of the sun—
and winding behind us, grottos of thought.

Charles H. Crump (1926–)

Raised in Rattlesnake, Idaho, "Charlie" Crump studied with A. Wilber Stevens at the University of Idaho. After moving to western Nevada, he worked in parole and corrections for over thirty years, retiring in 1988. His first book of poems was critically acclaimed in the *Los Angeles Times*, and many of his earlier poems appeared in *Life*, *Look*, and other magazines. He has recently returned to writing after a long hiatus, and is an active member and co-founder of the Ash Canyon Poets. He has given several readings through the Humanities on the Road lecture series and frequently works as a poet in the schools. Many of his poems are ballads, and his best readings are accompanied by guitar.

Old Roots. Carson City, Nevada: Hardwood Books, 1988.
Spectrum. Denver, Colorado: Big Mountain Press, 1955.

INTERLUDE

I lift the dripping bucket from the spring;
brace it on my leg, and pause to rest;
from rooted clouds a myriad carols ring;
a gray shape scurries to a secret nest.

A breeze, redolent of the ferny bed
from which I have aroused it, sighs and passes;
it tousles a tall milkweed's silken head
and ripples gently over shadowed grasses.

Abiding peace, a shimmering sword of grace,
knights my being, a new identity
bestowed on me from some ethereal place
of royal kinship in eternity.

The bail-full bucket bites my aching thigh:
Back to business. I am only I.

Stephen Shu-Ning Liu (1930–)

Stephen Shu-Ning Liu was born in Fuling, China, near the Yangtze River, the son of a hermetic painter of waterlilies. His grandfather, a poet and Mandarin scholar, taught him the Chinese classics. Before the Cultural Revolution, he left for San Francisco in 1952. In nearly four decades of hard work since that time, he has received numerous awards, published widely, and earned his Ph.D. in English from North Dakota University in 1973. He is the first Nevada writer to have been given a Fellowship in Creative Writing (1981–82) by the National Endowment for the Arts. Twelve of his poems were featured in *Seneca Review* in 1979; others have appeared in *Georgia Review*, *Western Humanities Review*, and *Texas Quarterly*. He spent one year translating *Dream Journeys to China* into Mandarin for its bilingual publication in China and the United States. Since becoming an American citizen in 1973, he has returned to his native China three times to write and to visit his sister and five brothers. For the past seventeen years he has taught English at Community College of Southern Nevada in Las Vegas.

Dream Journeys to China. Beijing, China: New World Press, 1982.

CONG XIN

Cong Xin, my little brother, left us
after he had seen nine springs.
It was morning, a sunny day,
the fields outside the windows
were green and full of joyful sparrows.

Then came the black-robe priests
with ancient instruments of music.
Days and nights they stood before a row
of haunting candle flames and sang
their scriptures with never changing
sleepy tune, as if they were asking
favors for my brother from gods in heaven.

After Cong Xin's soul was saved by
the blood of the red-ear roosters,
my father brought from the village a
paper carriage and house, with a paper
lantern and paper driver, and burned them
in the graveyard, in order that my brother
might find his way home in the night.
We burned, too, a thousand paper dollars,
so that he might have something to spend.
Lastly my mother burned a paper kite,
for my brother's favorite sport was to
fly a kite in the spring wind.

I saw my mother dry her eyes with a white
handkerchief. I heard my father groan
as he walked to and fro, biting his fist.
I watched the ashes dancing by the cypress.
I smelled the fresh earth and herbs.
I felt the chilly evening air; and I knew
we would go home and leave Cong Xin here
behind a stone. And the day he left us:
it was morning, a sunny day.
The fields outside the windows
were green and full of joyful sparrows.

ON BATS

By chance I visited the little zoo of D. H. Lawrence,
and came to the caged bat of black eyes and wings,
which, the Englishman thought, is a symbol
of happiness to the Chinese.
If my grandfather could hear this in his tomb,
he would turn and open his eyes and shout:
"No! Mr Lawrence, not the bats!
They stole our salt last night,
and left dung and urine in the jar."

It was in some cool summer evening, I remember,
when oil lamps in the hall burned low,
with doors closed we started bat-fowling.
The salt-pilferer flitted rapidly in great circles,
till my bamboo pole hit his head.
Like a piece of mud pie he dropped:
chi, chi, chi, he cried, tumbled and piteously died;
disclosing the tiny bag near his hairy belly,
we found a few drops of salt unconsumed.
My grandfather would, I know, chivalrously rescue
a moth from a spider, but care little for the bats.

MY FATHER'S MARTIAL ART

When he came home Mother said he looked
like a monk and stank of green fungus.
At the fireside he told us about life
at the monastery: his rock pillow,
his cold bath, his steel-bar lifting
and his wood-chopping. He didn't see
a woman for three winters, on Mountain Emei.

"My Master was both light and heavy.
He skipped over treetops like a squirrel.
Once he stood on a chair, one foot tied
to a rope. We four pulled; we couldn't
move him a bit. His licks could split
a cedar's trunk."

I saw Father break into a pumpkin
with his fingers. I saw him drop a hawk
with bamboo arrows. He rose before dawn, filled
our backyard with a harsh sound, *hah, hah, hah:*
there was his Black Dragon Sweep, his Crane Stand,
his Tiger Leap, his Cobra Coil . . .
Infrequently he taught me tricks and made me
fight the best of all the village boys.

From a busy street I brood over high cliffs
on Emei, where my father and his Master sit:
shadows spread across their faces as the smog
between us deepens into a funeral pyre.

But don't retreat into night, my Father.
Come down from the cliffs. Come
with a single Black Dragon Sweep and hush
this oncoming traffic with your *hah, hah, hah.*

I'M ENTERING YOUR SHADOW

I'm entering your shadow, in Huntington Park,
I can hear your footsteps in the bamboo grove,
you cough aloud as usual, in winter. I can see
you in the pond where lotus blossoms puff fire,
and I feel, in the last streak of the sun, your
painting brush twitching up and down, up and down
on every fence, every pole, every stone wall:

here's your humpbacked heron by the estuary,
where a fishing boat moored in the idling rushes;
I halt to read your Zen poems on the twigs
of a cinnamon tree. I'm sure you must have talked
with Henry Thoreau on the virtues of jackpines
and chrysanthemums; you must have spoken to him
in your elegant Chinese.

I'm entering your shadow, in mid-December haze:
and again, I smell rice wine on your breath.
The wind drowns out your cough as you chide me
for not living a life like a recluse's heir;
a cloud of camellia leaves falls and blankets us,
like a mandarin robe of jade, tenacious,
soothing, sadly cool to my bones.

A SICK ELEPHANT

A sick elephant,
the hunters say,
would start a journey,
tottering through
the southern woods,
until he comes to
that hidden pile of
his bones:
you hear him trumpet,
and you see him kneel
as if
for a ritual;
his trunk reaches
as he sags easily
to the ground,
choosing to lie
in the white blinking
of the aspens,
in the thus thus thus
of the cicadas,
in the suns of home.

IN DISNEYLAND

for Miranda

On the Columbus Ship we are to discover
America, through swamps and river gorges
where crocodiles, cougars and wolves
will not ambush us, those Apache arrows
will stay on the bow, savage dogs by the huts
will not bark; in the Haunted Mansion, walls
will not crack, lightnings will not strike,
squeaking ghosts have no spell to freeze us,
flying spiders eject no poisons, vampire bats
in the trees suck no marrow-bones.

As we hurry to the exit, the October sun
swells and bleeds his way into the sea.
Our Disneyland tour is nearly over, my girl.
The bus will leave us somewhere in the West:
the sky dims, the wind is up, the fog gains;
our safari has just begun.

NIGHT ON THE SEA

Ah the steam whistles
that sadden the travelers!
I go tonight
for a voyage,
a long voyage, alone.

Now dim, now far, gone,
lights on the Huangpu River;
farther, still farther,
stars in my native sky.
What night is tonight,
to leave my home
and my country, forever!

And the mist, the waves,
the departing ship
that cannot bear
the wanderer's grief.
I sing, I moan,
I sink and I flow
upon a storm-raging sea.

HOMECOMING FOR APRIL

You wake to the bloodiest month of the year:
newspaper says that farm dogs brought home
human hands from the desert. A man stabbed his
wife and child and left them bleeding on the floor.
But we'll find a shelter for you, April,
my little sparrow arriving in spring storms.

We're not too far from the riverbanks,
where your grandpa fished his red-tail carps.
We're not too far from the oak grove,
where snowy egrets established their colonies.
Evening winds swing at us, full of clover scents.
Clouds float about like golden pagodas.
Arise from your mother's arms, my girl.
Look at our garden in cherry blossoms,
listen to those swallows in the eaves.
I see window lights, I see a bright chandelier
in the main hall. The Door God leans over, smiling,
the phoenix gazes down from the lintel.
Old folks are out there to greet us:
a red carpet, they say, is for a son's arrival,
but a green one for a daughter.

On my right stands your grandpa in his best
garment as if he had come for a wedding;
hardly can he remove his eyes from your face
yet limp, yet yellowish at birth. On my
left sighs deep your grandma who lowers her
head. "Welcome home, April," she murmurs;
"I had sometimes wished you were a boy
to sustain our family line. Ah April, April . . ."

"Dry your eyes, Mother," I plead. "No harsh words,
although your proverb says that 'to store crops
for times of famine, to breed a son for old age.'
Such saying is now stale. Aunt Li, your sister, had
a son, the spoiled brat, the opium pit frequenter.
You had sons, but I left home before the Revolution;
Chung Chu was gone when you lay in bed, dying.
Remember those who made you a box-coffin, those who
dug you a mud bed in the cornfield. They were daughters,
daughters. Sons are like mountain hawks:
they grew up and hurried away, affected by evil stars.

Therefore, be content. Embrace your daughter-in-law
for her being kind to your son. Pour blessings on
April's head and see your own images in her forehead.
What would you say about the baby's mouth, Father?
Does it not remind you of the lily bud you used
to paint? Our child arrives in the year of the Horse.
A good sign. Heaven may send Spirits to protect us.

Rarely we have time to meet like this, dear folks.
Leave your tombs unoccupied at the hillside.
Morning will not come. No light breaks in the sky.
The rainstorm has hushed all roosters in the field."

ON QING MING FESTIVAL

Imagining this time of year, at the peak of spring,
in the high country of Fuling,
you see magpies graze in the cavities of sand stones,
you smell cow manure on the humps of earth,
you hear someone weep behind the aspens:
townsfolk have come to the hillside carrying food
to their ancestor's spirits, burning paper money
and paper servants and adding new stones and trees
to the graves collapsed in the last winter storms.

And down the valley of dark ferns you see a man,
quaintly dressed, bury his head in the moist furze,
shamelessly he sobs, crying out that his mother died
on her bones, he did not attend his father's funeral,
he has wandered a dark side of the distant street,
and has no face to see the sun . . .
But could these day sleepers hear him below the grass?
Could they see him rise, wipe his eyes, shuffle down
the road and leave his unburned paper coins fluttering
whitely in the massive bushes, like butterflies?

HOW ABUNDANT IS THE SPRING

How green are the oleander trees,
how flame-red the sun flares;
how lively are those swallows
dipping into the sea-blue skies;
how gray is his hermetic garment,
how solemn his ancient face;
how slowly my shadow toddles
beside him like an unsteady child;
not a gesture, not a word spoken,
when he halts, lilts his head,
and marvels at the honeysuckles
creeping over the windows, roofs:
how like a castle the house stands.

Does the mountain freshet soak
into the turfy tomb and saturate
his withered veins with blood?
Does the earth split, send him
up in the electric storms?

Does March wind bloom the hillside,
grow flesh on his frugal bones?
What gods descend the sanctuary?
What angels sing their hosannas
in the peach-and-apple croft?

How abundant is the spring,
how brisk, how luminous, how warm
and how good it is to rise with a dream
in a black night, from my cold desert bed.

REDONDO BEACH

In camps I slept better than crickets,
never dreamed a winter excursion by the sea,
but nothing seems steady this evening:
thoughts in my skull, blood in my veins,
nerve tissues over my stomach, lights on
these skeleton ships, jumpy wings against
a half-burned sky. Nothing seems familiar:
this gritty shoreline, this blurred wharf,
this gaped Pacific with a maniacal bounding,
with a ghostly growl . . .

"Tomorrow's events," I heard the hunters say,
"may be read in a sea turtle's backbone.
A mountaineer will find his way home if he
knows how to observe the plants and stars."
Somewhere along those redwood-cloaked ravines,
their dogs cheered me, their fire warmed me,
their roasted rabbits stuffed me. "We track
down only black panthers," their Chief told me;
"we'll climb the hills at dawn. Stay close,
my boy, lest the wolves grasp you by surprise."
In camps I slept better than crickets,
never dreamed a winter excursion by the sea:

no magic bones in sand, no plants, no stars,
in evening's thick mist nothing seems to fit:
clouds stalk in, diabolic, hairy as beasts,
last sunlight glitters dimmer than camp fires,
ships loom shorter than redwoods. When the winds
abandon the pier, when the sea lies marble still,
I seem to hear dogs at a rocky lair:
over the coast comes a soft calling from hunters
in their forest of unruffled graves.

William Abrams (1932–   )

Bill Abrams was born in Oakland, California. He moved to Nevada in 1968 and completed his Ph.D. in English at the University of Nevada, Reno, in 1972. He is a consultant at the State Department of Education in English, a champion of poetry and poets—particularly in rural Nevada—and coordinates the annual Piñon Poetry Festival for northern Nevada students. He organizes and publishes *Nevada Young Writers and Artists*, assists with the various state writing projects, and is a caretaker of literature in the schools. His poems have appeared in *West Coast Poetry Review*.

A MINOR CARVER

He carved a lifetime of puppets
And only one Pinocchio,

Yet I never heard complaints
Against the hugeness of the odds,

And never saw him abandon
His chisel or his knife,

Though absence of that passing magic
Sometimes caused his hands to ache.

Not that it was his hands, he used to say,
Showing them to me, huge and trembling.

Yet he couldn't help but feel that something
Had called out to magic and was heard.

When he died, I saw him
Where he fell—an unfinished smile

On his newest wood, hands
Eased out unfamiliarly at rest.

Elaine Dallman (1934–)

Born and raised in Sacramento, Elaine Dallman attended Stanford as an undergraduate and later received her Ph.D. at Southern Illinois University. For years, Ms. Dallman has edited the *Woman Poet* series on female poets from various regions of the country. She has taught at Southern Illinois University and the University of Nevada, Reno, and sponsored a conference on women and literature in Reno, where she lives. She has been a poet in the schools in California, Illinois, and Nevada. Her poems have appeared in *Seven Nevada Poets*, *Brushfire*, and other publications. Presently, she directs educational tours, most recently on jewelry as art.

A Parallel Cut of Air. San Francisco, California: Medallion Guild, 1991.

Editor in chief for the following regional anthologies:

Woman Poet—The South. Reno, Nevada: Women-in-Literature, Inc., 1991.

Woman Poet—The Midwest. Reno, Nevada: Women-in-Literature, Inc., 1985.

Woman Poet—The East. Reno, Nevada: Women-in-Literature, Inc., 1981.

Woman Poet—The West. Reno, Nevada: Women-in-Literature, Inc., 1980.

A PARALLEL CUT OF AIR

Your hand
curves out from
a parallel cut of air,

touches your hair to stop
falling motion.

The hair
pushed back to its curve,
you fade.

It is your trick
down the long years.
You pre-thought its detail.

I think about your hand.
I think how I let
you arrive:

Your moving is
compliant. A replica
perfect in its shape.

My mind is full of people.
Some move, some partly move.

TRAVEL, TEA, HOME

"Living with sickie
would drive anyone cuckoo,"
Auntie says, lifting and kissing
me. Strings of blonde hair
around her, she walks from
husband to kitchen. . . .

She serves tea. My eyes
fill with tears. My nose
runs. In sad air, my uncle
floats in a coffin.
My aunt floats around it,
skinny and cuckoo.
Two cousins eat gingerbread cookies.

Too tired to walk the driveway,
I float up-tree.
My mom is the greenest leaf,
my dad a supporting branch.
They lullaby quiet into my ears.

EACH TAKES ONE LEAF

By a river,
where townspeople banked up rocks:
three girls.

Their skirts shirred by a mother
who believes a harvest is
three girls, blue dresses.

One girl pulls her skirt lightly,
lets her knees
into river water.

The tree's leaves.
She and her sisters climb,
reach.

            Each
breaks off one leaf,
imagines her green spirit
will let her live forever.

IN HIS COMPARTMENT

On a transcontinental train,
Ibsen turns his head. His eyes follow
to see one of his characters
in a suit cloth of mist,
his skin a mist more than flesh.
Ibsen looks into those eyes as if
into a well.
He knows hundreds of characters.
The two men divide, parting through the
night of ink.
Ibsen re-reads manuscript pages, thinks,

"I wait for my bright one
with a face like a moon
in a mist."
He sees a silver haze
sleeve the compartment wall.
They sit side by side
to go far beyond.

James Hazen (1935–   )

Born in Boston and raised in Columbus, Ohio, Jim Hazen received his Ph.D. in English from the University of Wisconsin, Madison. He has taught at several universities, and in 1971 he became a member of the English department at the University of Nevada, Las Vegas. He is an associate editor of *Interim*, and his poems have appeared in *The Cape Rock*, *Maryland Review*, *Painted Bride Quarterly*, and *The Galley Sail Review*. He is one of the many fine poets at the university.

LET ME KNOW HOW YOU FEEL

I didn't know that jacket
turned you on—thought it was me
I gave it away and now I can't
get you to bed at all

hope the guy who bought it
for 50 cents from Goodwill
doesn't show up here.
We keep too many secrets.

Was it the corduroy
the cut, the lined silk
inside the sleeves or what?
the stuffed, square shoulders?

And you always tell me
get rid of your tired
your hungry old clothes
I'll never do that again.

AFTER THE TORNADO

Our power failed, started
failed again. The dark is final
an early dusk enshrouds familiar things.

We grope back up the cellar stairs
our voices whisper with the gloom
and cool of lower earth. This blue

and fluctuating dusk forgets
the wind, the hurtling freight
roars on to other destinations.

The child sleeps in laundry
our love's intact, your glance invites
what I see of it I like. We live again

and find a confidence in kitchens.
Our walnut pie-safe stands, deep-waxed
doors open for another century.

THE HELICOPTER

A criminal night, the police chopper overhead
homes in on guilt, its searchlight beaming
down a thick, straight stab of light

on the yellow underbrush of small sins. I douse
my cigarette and stand in my own back yard
waiting to be caught, thinking of larger failures.

And the high roar comes closer in the dark
of hovering engines—in fact, a slightly friendly
clamor—an eggbeater entering innocent yolks.

I stand beneath my olive tree, the helicopter
roams above the neighborhood, probing the night's
alarm, creating crimes where none had been.

Peering upward through the leaves, I watch
a moving, relentless light stir consciences
and hear the grinding wail of every guilt

rising in the sea's froth of minds, the tidal moan
of recollections. I at least am innocent this time
I say, I didn't rob that corner grocery store

nor steal my neighbor's car—see it there
parked silent. But the beam insists, hovers and returns,
the roar of engines, coming close, intensifies.

Dennis Parks (1936–   )

Born in Berea, Kentucky, where he lived until he was eight, Dennis Parks was raised outside of Washington, D.C. He founded the Tuscarora Pottery School in 1966, an internationally recognized institution, which he directs to this day. It is located about fifty miles outside of Elko in northeastern Nevada. Parks recently organized and led a delegation of American potters on a three-week cultural exchange with Soviet ceramicists. He is widely regarded as Nevada's foremost ceramic artist. His pottery has been exhibited throughout the U.S. and Europe. Ironically, he started his artistic career as a poet, studying with John Ciardi, and later attended Breadloaf Writers' Conference, where he studied with Robert Frost. After years of writing, he chose pottery as a way to make a living.

MY ANGEL CONTEMPLATES SIN

As you might read the crystal eye
My angel contemplates sin
In a manner not unlike
The act itself
The angel has no eyes but fists
Slab wristed square pounding
My angel contemplates sin
As you might kiss your brother
My angel contemplates sin
In a manner not unlike
The act itself
Her columning thoughts rounded
Raise dust with solid wings
My angel contemplates sin
As you might pocket your hands
My angel contemplates sin
In a manner not unlike
The act itself

Casual, at home, with her peers
Natural, out of necessity
My angel contemplates sin
As you might scribble I love wine
As you might scream with pain
                                        with joy
                                          with expectation
As you might shoot yourself
Loud, but by yourself
Hoping you might yet see a conclusion
Thoughtless, out of curiosity
Helpless, out of impatience
Wordless, out of knowledge
As you might construct an accident
Momentarily, unprecedented
Unique, odorless, forgotten
As you might live alone
After hours, pinching
To test your reality
As you might pry religion
Once a week and turning
Away because it never lasts
My angel contemplates sin
As you might shoot a spider
Testing your skill
On small life
As you might try your luck
My angel contemplates sin
In the loin of her wings
Beats her head round
Practicing
My angel contemplates sin
(Only when she isn't flying)
And is perched in the rear of my head
In a manner not unlike the act itself.

WHY WE SHOULD MAKE LOVE IN THE STREETS

The beautiful must be loved
Loved by you by me by all by God
By God she is sweeter than the Trinity
And three times lonelier the loneliest

One I ever met pinched my jewels
By the Gare de L'Est and spoke French
Running on so fast to catch her out of breath
I seized my knowledge counted to ten
And gave her the days of the week

In a broken meter I pounded
My little coffee bread of joy
And she clicked her long painted nail
To 4/4 time in the wedge of my baldness
By God I would have given my passport
For a taxi full of loneliness of that old vision

Of her awkward love where petticoats
Vaguely made all the difference in the sameness
Shout like the sea sound of the full
Gymnasium of your body it is it is it is

It was, once upon a life when tears
Made the man made the man
Know life was worth living in the street
If at all lovely if at all lonely
Open your door and go out

God knows it is no use keeping the still born
Too long at the breast children never realize
A parent's devotion regardless of love
Beauty is an act of trust.

ALWAYS

She scratched my name
under hers
On the ring in the tub,
Then kissed me in defiance.
It is all the same,
said she,
D.P. & E.C.
But she scratched my name on the ring in the tub
just under hers:
E.C.
D.P.
A splash was made as I took up a rag,
As we swirled
and sank
syntaxless.
Calm;
It is all the same,
said she,
And inserted her great toe for a stopper.

MEMORY IS A THIN PINE, OR MAYBE FIR

Once well remembered is better
Than behind every tree
All those leaves
Matted
humus.

And once well remembered
In the dark
Is illuminated.

Once is no city.

Once well remembered is better
Than always groping for her name.

Peter Parsons (1937–   )

Born in the Philippine city of Baguio, Peter Parsons attended Yale University, where he served as chairman of *Yale Lit* (he was one of the first editors to publish a poem by Mark Strand). After receiving a B.A. in English, he spent several years in the printing and publishing industry in southern California. Later, in Las Vegas, he published the *Nifty Nickel*. Though primarily a fiction writer, he has had both poetry and prose published in *Interim*. A father of five, Peter Parsons has returned to graduate school at the University of Nevada, Las Vegas, and divides his time between Las Vegas and Corona, California.

VILLANELLE

I saw him bold, I saw with bitter eyes
His face, him smiling off to war,
And now, the prey of birds, in fields he lies.

The story of his going lives and dies;
He was and is the child we can't ignore.
I saw him bold. I saw with bitter eyes

The day he left us in a rain of lies—
We'd hug and kiss again, "soon," we swore—
And now the prey of birds. In fields he lies . . .

We don't know where the fields or where the skies
That blanket him. Look, there in the door
I see him bold, I see with bitter eyes

The fleeting life he lived with us: it sighs
Across my heart until it sighs no more.
And now, the prey of birds, in fields he lies,

Something to disrupt, disorganize
Our lives, an endless pain that we explore.
I see him bold, I see with bitter eyes,
And now, the prey of birds, in fields he lies.

Ronald W. Manning (1938–   )

Raised in Wisconsin, Ronald Manning worked as a police officer in Los Angeles, San Francisco, and Oakland, California, before moving to Tonopah to become the graveyard-shift weather watcher at the Tonopah Airport. There he writes prose and poetry and tries to reconcile over twenty-one years spent on urban streets. Unlike that of many Nevada poets, his work is a narrative that quietly evokes the threads of rural and urban existence. It is no coincidence that these poems are filled with central Nevada moon and sand or the breath of the begging city. Primarily a fiction writer, he writes poetry because in it he "finds a separate and satisfying reward." In 1980 he received first prize for a short story in the Southern Utah State College literary magazine, *Tailwind*.

ANOTHER COP-KILLING

Dick Betts called me the oth
er day to tell me that Bob H
arris had swallowed his gun.
The funeral was in Sacrament
o and he wanted to know if I
wanted to go I said no and t
old him to call me when he g
ot back and we would paint t
he trim on his house He ne
ver called back I think he
misunderstood about the trim.

SATURDAY RAT SHOOT AND RIVER WALK

My paper route ended near the dump,
next to the river.

On Saturdays I took my Red Ryder
thousand shot Daisy
lever action carbine
with leather thong
and saddle ring.
There were rats
to be shot
at the dump.
The rats were tough.
But it's not true
that they charge
when they're wounded.

In the spring,
river paths,
like sunken graves,
have to be reclaimed
from the musty pack
of dead,
winter-pressed leaves.

A wild, brown river duck
waddles and flaps with a sudden,
great racket in the lapping shallows
near the river bank,
shamming a bad wing.
Her brash, splashing show
draws my attention away
from a hidden nest
I've accidentally threatened.
She slowly quiets as I pass on.

Ahead
red and blue and black and white
birds appear and
disappear and
reappear like iridescent popping corn
among the black tree trunks

and heavy, wet, green leaves.
They dip and weave,
chattering and bitching
at my intrusion.

Beside the path a sparrow,
fresh-dead and limp, hangs,
impaled on a rusty length
of forgotten, twisted
barbed wire.
Somewhere near, I sense,
a butcherbird watches and waits.
The world is full of sparrows.

Beyond the noisy green,
the musky stench
of river mud
and dead carp, with
bloated white bellies
at attention,
marooned,
in stagnant spring
pool remnants,
remnants shrinking,
taking life,
returning a grave.
Blue bottle flies
gather on their chests like medals
to honor the bodies of the dead.

Across the dome of the river
stand the estates of the rich.
Long green lawns stretch
from white-walled mansions
and drop quietly,
extravagantly,
to the river edge.

Well-kept sheds
straddle dock ends
and shelter expensive,
Chris-Craft speed boats.

Climbing back to the dump
a suitable can is selected
and kicked all the way home.

A LESSON IN PLOWING

He would mark the turn-around
with a great splash of tobacco juice,
and wave,
as he reset his course.

Lying in the hot, green weeds,
I watched the furrows open.
Wavering, wet heat
swallowed the tractor tires
and shimmered up his back
leaving just a head,
floating,
on distant noise.

The far turn-around
was my cue.
Squinting downfield,
I made my guess,
ran to the spot
and spat.

Tom Meschery (1938–)

Tom Meschery was born in Harbin, China, to Russian parents who fled Russia during the Bolshevik Revolution in 1917. Eventually, the family immigrated to the United States after the Second World War. As a boy, he tells stories of his father, a hulking man, weeping after reading Pushkin. From this background came a former NBA great (for the Golden Gate Warriors and Seattle Supersonics) and a poet of unflinching humanity. His book *Displaced Persons*, from which many of these poems come, is a narrative biography. Like Stephen Liu's longer poems, Meschery's are profound in their simplicity and at times horribly vivid with the struggle of immigration. His first book of poems was published at the height of his basketball career. He later went on to coach professional basketball, then took two years off to complete his M.F.A. from the University of Iowa. His poetry has appeared in *Antaeus*, *Iowa Review*, *Carnegie Mellon*, and *Northwest Poetry Review*. Meschery has worked as a poet in the schools in several small Nevada towns, and today teaches English at Reno High School. He is married to the novelist Joanne Meschery, and they make their home in Truckee, California.

Caught in the Pivot (essays). New York City, New York: Bantam Books, 1977.

Over the Rim (poems). New York City, New York: Saturday Review Press, 1971.

Father, you hardly speak in English.
When you try, it is
like a man losing his breath.
Always your hands trying to make sure.
Clenched fist meaning anger.
Thumb up, approval.
In confusion, your fingers

groping in the space between us.
Some signs I never learn.

When you fail
you return to Russian.
But I turn away.

Foreigners,
we live together
with no common language.

13

Our Saints look down over your shoulder
from their corner perch
shaking their beards,
angered by these foreign sounds:
Slap leather!
Dark collapsed over the prairie.

You put them there
where they could not climb by themselves.
Placed candles, lit them
and stood, head bowed,
as the priest shook incense.
You pay the rent.

Now, they scold you
for reading Zane Grey.
Slav, they're yelling, Slav!

But by then
your finger drops,
tired of following bewildering
words, and your eyes close.

I know you've gone back
to the West, where
men entered a new land
looking for a fresh start.

Drift Fence, Light
of the Western Stars,
Wanderer of the Wasteland.

Night after night, I watch
paperbacks slip from your hands
open, like tents, onto your lap.

11

Wounds do not heal.
Yours on your chest and legs purple in winter.
Running my finger along the edges,
I wish your silence
might become the story
that matches scars.

Something heroic
I can tell the kids at school
of Cossacks cutting
down Communists
especially for Mrs. Rose,
the math teacher,
who says all Commies are devils
and, then, makes sure
everyone in class
knows I'm a Russian.

MARIA VLADIMIROVNA LVOV 1917–1941

In Siberia the snow not only falls
from the sky, it grows from the ground.
When we looked back from the train
at graves we just dug for friends
or relatives, they were already white,
crosses like crystals.
If we touched the window frames, flesh
stuck. It was painful to free ourselves.

On the shores of Lake Baikal
we knelt, cupping our faces
against the ice to see ancient fish
trapped a hundred yards or so below
the frozen surface, scales
magnified as clear as fingernails.
While on the waiting train
impatient British and American
Red Cross missionaries
wondered about the strange
religious customs of the Russians,
still half uncivilized orientals,
stopping to pray to a lake
when at any moment Bolsheviks
might gallop out of the forest.

Your grandmother was a saint, she prayed
all the way to China. Your grandfather
said he was bound to return once we were safe
in Harbin. I could not think of anything
except the miles and miles of snow
our train was cutting through like scissors,
land like a sheet of paper
falling off behind us on either side
of the tracks—our lost lives.

My brothers were too young. They had
filled their pockets with their only history:
marbles, colored pencils, tin soldiers,
dreams no bigger than trinkets.

But I had already kissed a boy
and left him behind to kiss other girls
or to die kissing the cold ground.
Do you understand how such a small
embrace can be like a country?

Tom, nothing we lose can be replaced.
The closer to escape we came
the more we looked at the photographs.
I began to look beyond faces
to backgrounds: birches
clinging to river banks,
icicles hanging from our roof,
curtains, bannisters, the Afghan
rugs in papa's study
his samovar, the petit point
on mother's pillows, remembering
details as if without some moorings
people would float out of their pictures.

That's when our icons became more
to me than saints. I gave them
names: of the dead, of the four points
of the compass, the four seasons.
I held them for hours
stroking their beards, feeling in their weight
the comfort of a father's lap.

When we crossed the border
I counted who was left: your uncles
my mother, counting ourselves
lucky, knowing others would count on
only the air around their bodies.

Harbin was like a Russian city.
We built churches until all the family jewels
were sold off to the Chinese.
Then, I began to see counts drunk
or dead, countesses hurrying
for brothels in Shanghai.
Some nights, the younger men, bored
and full of vodka, slipped back
into Siberia to fight the Reds, as if
dying was the only job they could find.

I wept because my body was not strong
enough to comfort all of them, between
raising my little brothers, watching
my mother slowly dying. One boy, no older
than you are now, screaming he was a bird,
flew through glass. He was.
The broken shards on the sidewalk
looked like feathers in the sun.

Your father was one of those young men
without hope. He had watched his brother
tortured and shot to death in a jail in Russia,
escaped, fought with the army of Kolchak
across Siberia, only to be jailed
in China for refusing to turn in his guns.
I bailed him out. We married quickly.
Out of mutual kindness.
For most of us, all that was left
of passion was survival.

In '36 Militsa was born.
In '38 your birth almost killed me.
How strange, I thought, to survive
such dreadful conditions
only to die of love.
Your father left in '39
for America. We couldn't leave

until '41, December seventh
a week too late. You know the rest.
Except this: the day I left Russia
when I was seventeen, I knew no matter
where we went, I would always be displaced.

33, NEW YORK, EASTER, 1983

I haven't thought of you seriously
for years, not since browsing
through a bookstore
I came across photographs of you
in a bound collection.
Even then, your faces
seemed more like Chippendales
or rare tapestries,
articles with an appraised value.

Until tonight, fulfilling a promise,
I led my teenage daughters
into a blaze of golden faces,
icons, one of you for every candle,
halo after halo.
I almost fainted.

And might have, if my daughter
hadn't whispered, dad,
there's Baryshnikov.

Dapper in a tailored suit
next to a mink, next to another mink,
next to a blue fox. What kind
of Russians are these, I thought?

Saints, you've come a long way
from San Francisco. Are there no
babushkas in New York? No Tartar eyes,
broad faces with high cheek bones?
Old men wearing ill-fitting double breasteds?
No kneeling here, floor
rising up, foreheads bending down,
endless three fingered crosses?

Saints, you who always looked
so ancient to me, look younger
suddenly out of context
in New York. Ministering to this flock
of *Haute Couture,* your wrinkles
have faded, your beards
are no longer as long or as white
as in my childhood memories of whispering
confessions into snow.

When exactly was it during these years
while I was away that you left,
en masse, to come to the "Big Apple?"
Became Americans, like me.

John Garmon (1940–   )

A Texan from the start, John Garmon was born to farming parents on the Texas panhandle, near Amarillo. One of eight brothers and sisters, he joined the marines, then started college at twenty-six. He received his Ph.D. in English from Ball State University. He has taught at numerous colleges throughout the country. When he arrived in western Nevada, he founded the Ash Canyon Poets (along with several others), the Western Mountain Writers' Conference, and later, Hardwood Books. The Writers' Conference hosted many important poets and fiction writers over the years, and it is a tribute to Garmon's vision that it took place at all. His work has appeared in such publications as *Commonweal*, *Southern Humanities Review*, and *Southern Poetry Review*, as well as numerous chapbooks. Few people have done more in such a short time than John Garmon to bring writers and writing to western Nevada. After returning to his native Texas, he accepted a position as the dean of instruction at Yavapai College in Prescott, Arizona, where he lives today.

Llano Sons: Trips and Passings (co-authored with Jim Harris and Tony Clark). Hobbs, New Mexico: Hawk Press, 1989.

Dust in My Teeth. Pueblo, Colorado: Academic and Arts Press, 1989.

Mornings After the Nativity. Muncie, Indiana: Ball State University Press, 1976.

GROWING UP WITH THE DRUNKS ON HIGHWAY 66

they came in thirsty from oklahoma
mostly skinny farmers barely able
to clothe themselves with that aroma
of bathless months and a meager table
and guilty depression eyes
as if a government's mistakes
had bottled up their cloudless skies
and given them the shakes
as if they couldn't realize

how easily a bottle breaks
how liquor never cuts the dust
and drinking cannot heal
the hurt that richer men may trust
they got the short end of the deal
my father said
some would work and some would steal
and some would be found dead
one frozen under a winter fence
another who had gone wrong in the head
and cut himself in haste
to stop the cruel tigers of his thirst
those wild creatures who chased
the dryland farmers who were cursed
and had no abundance but weeds
and broken families
with sunken eyes and needs
no drinking men could please

THE MORMONS

thinking jesus and joseph smith
burning in the light beaten the mobs
in all that low river country where corn
grew fat as cactus they struck the wheels
handcarts against the rocks
and left buzzards bone with flesh
a path of circling black birds
crazily swimming through alkali meadows
those women bore and bore their men
and the babies and the dead came
stalking a new terrain a rattlesnake's eyes
flaring from ever' scrub of sage
and no tabernacle but the vault of clouds
no giant pipe organ whose spires grow needles
and sound only a toneless hymn to a hot heaven

circled with scavengers
the hard faces even of children their great eyes
reaching from above skin taut over young cheekbones
to focus on a faith of their elders

FROM CASPER TO CHEYENNE

ride the swooping bus over indian artifacts
packed under the centuries of thin topsoil
over the muddy hills through sandstone cragways
through muddy gap or glendo all the same places
wide places by the ridiculous road and the hills
give way far off to mountains the sky is eating
under the purple canopy of wyoming dusk
emptiness walks the littered aisle of the sleek bus
cruising like a great whale surfaced and lost
flowing with the gravity of the landscape
through the windy curves and over the bouldered hulks
where spring comes but accidentally and colorado
hangs down there green all the way to denver
where the yellow giant beetles who chew into wyoming
spawn and yearn for black glittering food
under the indian artifacts

TEXAS DADDY

there you are a young man
framed against the barbed wire
tumbleweeds at your feet
your dark wavy hair innocent in
the youthful eyes of your
thirty years manhood the rock
your children anchored to

a prometheus in overalls
your gaunt face is full of hope
it denies the great depression
refutes the black noons of those
dry days of fearful eyes
and ghosts of nerves skittering
in ditches along the rutted roads

then you were that peach-fuzzed
hope magistrate ruling our destinies
hardly sure of yours
the rains came and mother lived
the days of your youth drifted
to a fencerow made sturdy with rain-fed weeds
fields blossomed
your sons and daughters came of age

now you walk along the widening modern ditches
the vast plains sweep out to distance
a shadow behind you follows fills fades forgets

SUMMER COLORED GIRL

you in your long golden
legs in your green bikini
in the pink grapefruit breasts
glazing the blue space
under this yellow sun

you in your red liquid
movements framed in white
beach towels sprawled out
opening tulip orange
to meet air kissing

you in your long cinnamon
hair wisping out fanlike
against the brown sand
in the deep gray warmth
this summer twilight brings

ALL DAY WEEKDAYS

All day in the peeling office
under the ceilings of leftover wars
in the old barracks at the university
through curtains the sounds of cars
come in to frighten dreams.

And this is the goal of knowledge
to breach the beaches of books
and storm the bastions of words
until the enemy gives.

One day is one of a week
and fifty-two a year
of years which bring degrees
which bring lack of vision.

And people walk the days
down the weeks of halls
and carry important volumes
and grow beards and look solemn
and speak to directors and deans
and complain to department heads.

All day the days of the weeks
the weeks of the years of the earth
the stubble of uncut lives
the absence of wholesome sin

we could have committed once
before this knowledge set in.

GOOD-BYE TO MY COWBOY UNCLE

You poked fun at my fat.
One summer as a visitor
I heard you beat my cousin
your son for crying
when a horse kicked him.
I listened from another room.
You used a cowboy belt
wide with leathery pain.

My mother your sister
wondered why I would not go
to your ranch anymore.
I did not attend your funeral.
I stopped all visits
when I saw your real face
that day at the creek
when you threw the burlap
bag containing kittens.
"It's nature's way," you said.

I hear your smoking got you
and that daily whiskey helped.
You were a Marlboro Man.
You hated sissies who cried
and fat kids from the city.
You liked to twist my arm
to see how long I'd stand it.
You liked to laugh at tears
when I wept at your tactics
breaking horses that summer.

Their mouths bled. They fell
to their knees under you.

Are you to ride herd somewhere?
Bring cattle down from grazing
on the high summer grass?
There aren't too many like you
these days of ease. I know.
Your son my cousin beat you
to the grave, drunk and speeding
around that curve of two-lane
into a herd of steers.
They told me you shed tears.
I find that hard to believe.

FAILURE

When I wanted to reach you, Brother,
older brother, that night in the dark
as you wept in the top bunk, I lay
choked on darkness, thinking, "Failure.
He didn't make the team." I could not speak.
Your bitterness might have been eased by strangling me.

"You are *not* a failure!" I wanted to shout,
but I chewed on the salty sheet instead
and heard your sobbing out. You did not know
I knew. You told Mother at supper,
"I'm a failure, I didn't make it, I'm lousy."
She trembled, tried to stop your woe, your words.
But you jumped up, stumbled tear-blind to bed.

I came in later, playing I thought you asleep.
But I lay there a long time listening to you weep.

Elizabeth I. Riseden (1940–)

A native of Ely, Nevada, Elizabeth Riseden has written prose and poetry for over twenty years. After finishing her M.A. in English at the University of New Mexico, Albuquerque, she taught at Western Nevada Community College and the University of Nevada, Reno, and later became a social worker in Reno. Her first novel, a fictional account of life in Virginia City during the late 1800s, was published in 1982. Her poetry has appeared in *Sand Mountain Forum*, *Brushfire*, and *Facets*. Today, she lives and works as a massage therapist in Carson City.

Frontier Dynasty (novel). New York City, New York: Zebra Press, 1982.

OLD WOMAN IN COLD

I fear for you
    on a night like this,
        5 degrees at 5 o'clock
            with Christmas traffic
    assaulting your village street.
I fear for you
    with cold in my heart
        when you tell me of pain
        and the pain's not just
            in your joints as you,
Child of wagon-drawn desert
    solitude,
Try to adjust yourself, on crutches,
To a town of 50,000 where once
    50 was a crowd.
I'd take you to me, but
    you wouldn't take it.
Even now, in your amber light, you
Continue to teach me, though
You need my holding.

Robert Dodge (1941–)

Born and raised in Cincinnatus, New York, Robert Dodge received his Ph.D. from the University of Texas at Austin. He moved to Nevada in 1970 and has been on the English faculty at the University of Nevada, Las Vegas, since that time. He has written novels, several short stories, and his poetry has appeared in the *Chariton Review*. He co-edited two Native American poetry anthologies (right). (The word *Wah'kon-tah* is variously translated as great spirit or being.)

Early American Almanac Humor. Bowling Green, Kentucky: Popular Press, 1987.

New and Old Voices of Wah'kon-tah (co-edited with Joseph McCullough). New York City, New York: International Publishers, 1985.

Voices from Wah'kon-tah (co-edited with Joseph McCullough). New York City, New York: International Publishers, 1974, 1976.

WEIGHT WATCHERS

I

Surrounded by fat women,
I sit in my creaking chair
Listening to our leader
A woman who lost seventy pounds
More than two years ago
Telling about the time she ate
All the leftover bread pudding
At her restaurant.

She used a large serving spoon
And shoveled it into her mouth
Hardly chewing it all, swallowing
Until it was all gone. We laugh. She smiles.
We're supposed to feel appalled

And sympathetic, but it brings back
Sweet memories.

II

Next door to Weight Watchers
The Swiss Cafe offers Medallions
of Beef, Spaetzle, Blue Cheese Dressing
And Chocolate Mousse Cake.
Sometimes the smell from their
Kitchen drifts into our room.

III

My father cooked steak on the backyard grill,
Twice as much as we could eat, red in the middle,
Dripping with juices. My mother made rolls.
Everyone agreed hers were the best rolls in town.
For dessert we ate raspberry pie. Each of us had
a quarter of it. I've never eaten better.

IV

Before our meeting, each of us steps on the scales.
More than two percent of me is gone.
Sometimes I think there is a constant amount
of human fat in the world. When someone loses weight
It floats in the air waiting to grasp another person.
It prefers people who are already heavy. Fat
Attracts fat. My six pounds hovers over our group.

V

In fact, I know my six pounds burned away.
Expelled as carbon dioxide and water
In the slow process of human combustion.
Still, fat hovers in this room. Two women
Wear ribbons proclaiming they've lost ten
Pounds or more. Our leader lost seventy.
Others have lost. I feel the weight pressing
And suffocating. Waiting and watching.

VI

As I leave the meeting, I open the door to
The Swiss Cafe, and let it in.

Bill Cowee (1942–   )

Born in Milwaukee, Wisconsin, Bill Cowee grew up in Montana and graduated from Absarokee High School. He later attended USC where he received his B.S. in business and worked as a comptroller for a major grocery chain in southern California for twenty-three years, writing all the while. Five years ago he moved to Mound House, Nevada. A founding member of the Ash Canyon Poets and for two years, a principal organizer of the Western Mountain Writers' Conference, Cowee's poetry has a voice all its own. Some of the poems below come from a series about American Flat, a mining camp on the Comstock. His poetry has appeared in *South Florida Poetry Review*, *Calapooya Collage*, *Interim*, and others. Along with Charles Crump, he has given several readings in the Humanities on the Road lecture series to much acclaim. As with many who work in separate careers, Bill Cowee's poetry is a nighttime preoccupation. During the day he is an accountant in Mound House.

DRIFTING

We are the song death
takes its own time
singing.
—Robert Hass

Each Sunday in church, we've watched
stiff shocks of white hair tumble
across your forehead, listened
to you cough on the hissing oxygen.

The rusting process, oxidation,
bubbling life gasses through decay,
through the cancerous quicksand
of your once erect body, now slumped

a Macy's balloon after the parade.
Where are you drifting, Charlie?
Can you see an afterlife behind eyes
withdrawn from your vacant face?

You hardly rustle, stealing away
before our choir-loft stares;
this Sunday a little less mouth
around the Communion host,

less recognition in recited prayer,
less strain on the taffy muscles
pulling oars to another life.
The fallacious immediacy of death

slowly stretches to a material-
spiritual transparency before
eyes readily misting. Will we hear
your soul snap, torn on its parting?

Or, one day, discover faint husks,
dry fingers wrapped on the oak pew
like translucent cicada shells
cling to the church foundation?

MEETING GANDHI ON THE MARKLEEVILLE ROAD

Beneath the cloud-spewing mountains
driven by wind-gusted breath
the uprooted brush tumbles,
tangles along the fence line.

Wild grass grown thick
rustles on hidden ditch lines,
broadens to pheasant freeways
in the aging Sierra autumn.

Green hay is baled and stacked;
fields now smooth fresh sheets
washed and spread with anticipation
of winter's first heavy snow.

Near the field's marshy end
handfuls of granite boulders lie,
headstones scattered in a graveyard
where fingers of an Ice Age glacier

slipped their burden and expired.
Further, in a fallow field near Minden,
astride the freeway easement,
stands a massive cottonwood

watching a new roadbed travel south
toward the ringed target in its trunk.
I think of Gandhi, sitting resolutely
on the tracks of the Calcutta railway,

passively in the path of England.
As yellow flowers and Gandhi's ashes
once floated slowly down the Ganges,
leaves fall, tumbling along old asphalt.

THROUGH LONG WINDOWS

You were horse, you . . . dammit,
        Get up! Pull your softening bones
from the Comstock sand, from beneath
        drifted soil where purple lupine
bloom through the long windows
        of your rib cage.

Wild Nevada, woven
in unkempt mane, the wind now curries free
        through swatches of sorrel horsehide
left by scavenging coyotes, hawks.
        Chattering magpies stuff coarse tail
hair in the mattress of their nest.
        Rise!

Collect your shattered teeth,
pull back your upper lip, laugh
        cheat grass breath into his face,
as well you must have, before
        the bastard blew your nose
through your brain and out . . . blood
        splattering his shotgun.

Trample
sun-cracked hooves on his chest,
        shorten his breath, as killing held
air still for a horrible second
        as victim and murderer die.
You were mustang, damn you,
        Get up!

STEAM BELLIES AND CHEAP COIN

I filled mountain ears with the screech
of steel, shrill Virginia & Truckee whistle,
tubercular chuff of pressured steam.
I blinded hawk's keen sight with tamarack
smoke, rattled pine nuts in a crow nest
hummed your miner's song of silver.

I hauled you to the mines, sold you,
shook you from your restless sleep
and dragged you into the Brother's War
into greed, bright falls of tailing waste
stamp mills, cave-ins, hells stewing
with bad air and mine chemicals.

I coaxed you from the rough thighs
of the brothel queens, down the squared
stopes to the two-thousand-foot level
where you labored against the heat five
minutes before retreating into the chill
pneumonic dampness of the icehouse.

I watched you spend your life recklessly
cheap coin tossed on the faro table,
tumbling down the sluice of saloons—
Brown's, McCarthy's, Nesbit's, the Willows—
like a drunken nugget of nocturnal gold
until snatched by the baffles of your tent.

I gathered you in when the highgrade
played out; sheltered you, prodigal son
and led you from this land of promises—
Gold Hill, American City, Lousetown,—
returned you to California fields and rivers
where the digs and the dreams still lie.

STILLWATER REFUGE

". . . risk is full:
every living thing
in siege . . ."
—A. R. Ammons
"Corson's Inlet"

Dawn. A ghostly rustle
of snow geese in grass recalls
the shuffling reeds woven
by forgotten basket makers.
An old promise of ponds
echoes along the Pacific flyway.

Green mallard and cinnamon teal;
the rust of ruddy duck flashes
from nearby fields of millet, wheat.
Long flights south pause
in these wetlands where
Canadian geese rest, restore.

Tired mother of Nevada lakes
Lahontan's Pleistocene water stills
ages muddled beneath a toxic veil.
In solutions of irrigated desert salts
stirred with selenium and mercury,
cultures of avian botulism survive.

Under the hostile stress of drought
egrets and avocets refuse to nest
abandon their clutch of eggs
die wandering in the bulrushes.
Fish float to the surface
gill slits open, silent lips
in suffocating air, helpless
as afternoon winds sweep
them into ragged silver
ribbons of false shoreline.

Along charcoal and tawny sand
a black-necked stilt, content
on its brittle walk of secrets,
stalks grasshoppers, stalks
while the stealthy marshes
the wetlands, close
curl inward on themselves,
the ancient wetlands
shrinking in.

Joan Cutuly (1942–)

A native of Detroit, Michigan, Joan Cutuly was raised in Clairton, Pennsylvania. She received her M.Ed. from the University of Pittsburgh and taught English at Robert Morris College for three years before relocating to the West Coast. A Las Vegas resident for the last ten years, she currently teaches English at Clark High School. Not surprisingly, much of her poetry is steeped in that experience and she has recently completed a book-length poem on teaching, *Home of the Wildcats*. She is a gifted poet who brings an enthusiasm for literature and poetry to her students, which is singularly unique. Her poems have appeared in *Bristlecone*, *Pivot*, *Hyperion*, and *Interim*. But the real wonder is that she writes, reads, and conveys her love of literature to her students every day. She is the 1990 Hiram Hunt Poetry Award winner, presented by the English department at the University of Nevada, Las Vegas.

HYPOTHERMIA

The sun left us
to shadows of the narrow red canyon,
the river winding itself blind
no longer the lyrical power
hugging my legs
but a stony green rush
I slipped again
my shins already like split plums
thoughts caught in notches
too quick   to think
I felt grey
maybe some food
the bread stuck like wood
but I couldn't take any more water
its thunder like rocks falling from the stars
my mind was going under

we paused on a beach of flood stones
each to choose between small white fall and
still black pool
I waded into the silence
an invisible current pressed against me
my pack weighting back
the shiny wall   gripless
I dug my walking stick into the bottom
and with the fierce miracle of desperation
heaved myself free of the undertow

a wooded trail led around the next rapid
my skeleton radiated cold
every motion   a separate deliberate
thought   descending into a long
churning stretch   I rattled all over
we stood looking for a way through
that could not exist until tomorrow

on the last high ground
we built a fire of driftwood
box elders
like leafy branches of the canyon's heart
kept the light
from those fleshless edges
of our human endeavor.

MORNING GLORY

They recline in white and aqua deck chairs.
Two large blueberry muffins round out of themselves
On white China plates
From two mugs of herbal tea one stem rises
Easy as a Sunday going nowhere.

"Morning Glories," he says,
"Are the one tradition I've kept around here."
The phone rings.
In his absence, she is drawn
To the heart-shaped leaves climbing into the Junipers,
Blossoms blue as the holiness of all opening,
Centers like a child's happy sun.
She wanders across the yard of abstracts,
Bent metal, rounded pipe,
Dried agave secured with gauze—
This wife left less than the absence of flowers
But enough.

He finds her by the swimming pool clear as not water,
About to dip into the stillness of his trees.
He kisses into her bright yellow center.
"Come," he says, returning them to the muffins and tea,
Skirting her violet edges.

KEYHOLE CANYON, NEVADA

Come, quiet as the sun
visit the little long ago men
something in them burned
though they had no hope beyond
the protection of this brown canyon
they drew what they knew
as themselves
without mirrors
seeing what happy children think
open palms
wonder arms
jumping legs
heads like full moons
with no complication of face

snakey lines
amazing circles
herds like gods
no particular aim
past counting or praise
no technological bent
shaping these little long ago men
they were their own mythologies.

SACRED DATURA

"Open," whispers the dark of the canyon's heat.
Slow moonlight flowers from her tight fingers,
Shadows of stone casting without sin
On her violet-edged consent
Remembrance of trader   priest   trapper
Baskets of bone hands
Shards of mud hearts.
Silver deer walk toward water
Through the dry grass
About her deep green madness.
Footsteps in The Sea of Tranquility
Remain windless.
Her day always belongs to some future place.

THE SMOKERS

One step beyond the school's right to them
They light each other up
Hair-hanging easy dudes
Thin in faded concert shirts
        Sin after Sin
                KINGDOM COME   Reign in Blood

Say Aah and Ram It Down
Books dropped at the
curb in onomatopoetic
Fuck it
Backs to their alley, a 7-Eleven graveyard
Of Big Gulps, Twinkie and frozen burrito wrappers
Shoulders curving like dark question marks
Into their tight
Buttoned-up
501 balls.

BRANDON

I could have killed you more than once—
Always talking out,
Wandering the room,
Tearing off my pencil eraser
To hold your earring that lost its back,
Then just as the class dipped into Walden
Sporting your little key chain man
With penis that flipped up and down,
Pulling the knife behind my back.
I met your parents over that.
"Don't you want to be a good son?" the dean asked.
Your mother said despite braces and contacts
You never got over buck teeth and glasses.
Your father said he traveled so much.
I sympathized but wanted order.
You complied with the quiet of mountains
That take forever to die
And worked hard for a week.
I think of your fine movie star features
Plastered back and made up for the casket.
The day before you died, the class split for a debate:
"Do women mistake politeness for rights?"
"Brandon belongs with the girls," Roy said.

"Oh yuk!" squealed the girls.
"Jokes," they maintained. "Sorry," they said.
Usually you'd throw a book or sulk
But that day just stared, having begun, I think,
To empty your head of all assigned roles.
The next day the silence of the class so deep
No voice or hand could reach it—
Only one bewildered by the grief,
Our Vietnamese refugee
Recalling his neighbors murdered in the streets
By men he shot to save his father.
Within weeks he would be the butt of gibes
For having eaten dogs to stay alive.

Brandon, we are the questions
You answer
Buried with your Wildcat spirit button
Pinned over your breast.

TEACHER

for Joe Grucci (1911–1982)

I am hiking high on the edge of snow
the afternoons here are always prismatic
clear piñon light
fracturing off
the shatter of limestone
settling below
into the silent indigo elegance
of basin and range   basin and range

I nearly drove up the valley for this poem
into the hot maze of rock
where Old Mouse eluded enemy troops
that crafty Paiute knew like you
the secrets of water

I would have read your heart
in those simple faceless geometries
of stone etched
arms lifted high
in search
and praise
you were a hunter
and gatherer
those images would have worked
but it was your unwritten silence
that stood for me
the way vast mountains wait
you believed
and gently
broke my light.

WEDNESDAY, NOVEMBER 16, 1988
11:45 A.M.

Someone has taken the clock
From the English Department Workroom,
The rebel Accutrex that suddenly began running in reverse
To the bell order of students who never get any older
Or wiser.

Three years ago I requested a lectern
Which was ordered
Put on back order
Arrived
Got lost in The Warehouse
Had a tracer put on it
Actually wasn't ordered
No, was in fact ordered but
Delivered to the wrong school
"Not a good teaching tool anyway,
You'll get behind it

And lose touch with your students."
Was however reordered
Though not in this year's budget so
Will really be ordered
Next year
Which was last year

But within days, the clock . . .
It had hurt no one
We all have watches
I could have taken it home,
Let it run,
Delighted in its foolish inconsistency . . .
My brave clock, I should have known
They would take you,
Leaving only a blue painted-over screw
Waiting for the right time.

Billie Jean James (1942–   )

Born in Illinois and raised in Wyoming, Billie Jean James came to southern Nevada in 1970. She lives in the desert outside of Las Vegas and much of her poetry is rooted there. She has worked as a poet in residence for the Nevada State Council on the Arts and lectured frequently on creative writing. Her first manuscript of poetry, *Sandset and Other Poems*, was a finalist for the Walt Whitman Award in 1978 and 1980. Her work has been published in a variety of periodicals, including *Seneca Review*, *Wisconsin Review*, and *Contemporary Quarterly*. From 1983 to 1986 she lived in Saudi Arabia. After a period of inactivity and long reflection, she has once again returned to writing. She is one of several southern-Nevada poets who have carved a literary niche for themselves, despite the apparent isolation of living and writing in that environment.

HANDGRIP

I glimpsed you publicly
on monuments.
Every village
high in the mountains
or close to the sea
lists fathers
by brothers
dead from a gun.

I saw you stand erect
by statues and tombs
in the capital city.

When I walked once
with a boy
through the graveyard
so our parents
would not see us kiss,
you lay near some trees.

With wet eyes
I brushed by you
at movies
and inside my books.

One morning
with sun
outside the door,
we finally meet.
Unasked
you grasp
my fingers.

I look
on your empty face
and know each line
I never could see.

Every night
you come now
to my bed.

As I lie down
you reach out
ignoring tears.

Your cold hands,
Death
chose my young son.

DECAY

Sand flings handfuls at your trunk,
gray too long where no sap runs.
Twigs snap
on your stiff back.
Stand, Tree, another storm.

Scrape of branch
rattles bark
falling off
chunk by chunk.

Even insects leave this home.
An ancient web straggles,
some frayed thread.

Wind never moves deadwood back.
Limbs must be live
to push toward sun.

No bend nor curve
of green leaves
bursts from each node.
Tree, to your wintered face
the mouth of spring
brings no kiss.

WHOREHOUSE

The route marker tells my age. I'm 95.
Tonopah is halfway home. The mines all dead.
North Nevada's fields done; green is gone.
I see one hundred miles and not one tree.
These mountains all stand bald, though surely,

a brush of mesquite hides one wash.
Cat's claw has hooked some sand somewhere.
Girls live out here. SHERRI'S COTTONTAIL RANCH
open 24 hrs. like Vegas. ASH MEADOWS. Knights
ride up in pickup trucks, park with loaded pockets.
The owner keeps a gun for drunks. Don't bring
your gal. We serve single drinks. Back from the road
outside Mina I see BILLIE'S DAY NIGHT. A sign
on the desert. What water caused this nearby edge
of green? Such plants scarce. An old rusted tank
knocked over says WIDE LOAD. Mountains behind
are mostly gray. A shadow lines the top of her cheap roof.

PRIMER

In long grass
the neighbor boy
hissed
take down
your pants.
I thought
I heard
his strange word
again
when my mom
said *fought*.
I was afraid
but could not tell
nor ask.
In our backyard
before I ever
started school
I hid a piece
of snakeskin
inside a box

with my red bead,
a shell,
and turtle bone.

HOMING

Having highways all alone
west and south I come
returning to stars.
Sky had been too full of fog
but now the moon pulls near.
The first Joshua near Goldfield
stands like an old miner's ghost
welcoming me back to dust.
Drier and wider now this night
asks me to remove my sweater and stay.
The desert is home.

HOMESTEAD

Murphy's wife,
Sedda,
would stay
all winter
more quietly
than Wyoming's
first snow.

No fever
inside her cabin.
Wild rose hips
are dried for tea
after she remakes the floor
and lines log walls

with Grandfather's books,
chokecherry jam,
and paintings,
bright Indian feathers
for the war dance.

No bulls will break fence;
the new horse
throws no one
in winter.
Like some women
fold lace
Sedda splits wood.

Blue sky
settles down
white-cold
in a basin
above the Big Horns.

Cold drops lower.
The beaver goes
under his dam.
An early storm
sneaks into September
and takes leaves
just going gold.
Cottonwood and aspen
turn, dead-brown
to hang until
some cutthroat wind
happens across
from the plains.

As a girl, Sedda
helped men count skulls
in the canyon
after the blizzard.

Like an old squaw
she scouts birds
overhead till December
when horses and Herefords
still bawl out
from her snowbanks of sleep.
Sedda reads winter
in her dog's coat.

KINSHIP

Come, little feather,
before the sun screams
we must walk
out in the desert.

I want you to climb
with me to the mound,
my place on top
of white stones.

We will stand and turn
each direction.
Like Indians, look
to the mountains

under clouds
building to storm.
Thunderheads.
Talk softly.

Sit here so that owl
on the yucca
will not hear us
and fly.

Young one,
you will be gone
back to your home
before the rains come.

That eye looking
over Sunrise Mountain
will hide angry.
You will not see

this valley
wear its dark cape.
You will not hear
every stream

chased down the sides
of Mount Charleston.
Far away, niece,
you must wait

like dried seeds
in the ground
for spring to push
wildflower petals

up to the wind:
nama, verbena
and dock.
Come back again.

Follow your aunt's path
through the desert.
If it's been a wet year,
watch out for snakes.

SUPPERS

Graybeard musicians circle the table
with worn-out American songs
she does not want to hear in Milan.

I have to come back, Mary says,
to see the graveyard of statues
and the Romanesque church.
Doors closed on *The Marriage*
of the Holy Virgin. I shall return
like unhurried cats at the end
of that big castle's moat.
I will not climb up cathedral passages
quickly as schoolboys
chased by their friends.
Next time I must look longer
at centuries of rooftops.

Uncovered bread grows stale,
she notes, rustic for tourists
from the hotel next door.

Eating cold meats, roasts from the oven,
chicken after pasta, too much soup,
fish, potatoes, and eggs,
Mary feels overstuffed
as cannelloni.

She complains to her friend,
Tonight it rains food, Leonardo,
and you want me to eat
all of the courses.

Regional gifts I cannot accept.
Cheese nor fruits. No pears.
No red-meated oranges.

Such sweets, ices and cakes,
but Dear One, I am full.
Do not pour thick coffee,
she tells the waiter.
Bring no liqueur.

If another war comes, she thinks,
do not find me here
surrounded by plates.
Leonardo, let me be in your streets
you call gray.

Let me just stand near the stone monk
over a fountain with rain dripping
down my face.

Late tonight after this feast
she must write to her father:
At last I am here.
Yes, I, just an infant,
when you flew the metal stomach
packed full of bombs.

She must tell him how she stood
this afternoon in front
of da Vinci's *Last Supper*,
a wall left by others rebuilt,
at the church of Santa Maria della Grazie,
Mother of Favors.

No, she decides, I will not tell him
how I pulled my coat over the U.S. Bookshop's
too bright, red with blue, plastic, striped sack.
Miracle frescoes left upright
amid once-broken rafters and bricks,
she can describe, and the old photographs.
Black and white of forties' rubble

with children nearby
not much older
than she must have been.

Now Mary leans over like that disciple
next to the redeemer, Please, Leonardo.
No more.

She remembers again
her whispers inside the church:
Please, please
do not let my father
have been in that plane
which almost destroyed
the table of Christ.

Ursula Carlson (1943–   )

Born in Aluksne, Latvia, and raised in a West German refugee camp until the age of six, Ms. Carlson immigrated to Greenville, Michigan, as a girl and moved to Nevada in 1974. For her Ph.D. dissertation, she translated work by Latvian novelist Anslavs Eglitis. Most recently she translated Estonian novelist Arved Viirlaid. A short-story writer, essayist, and poet, she volunteers as a writer in her son's school in Carson City. Presently, she is writing a series of essays on Latvia, and last summer she returned to her birthplace to see her native land for the first time—a journey she thought would never take place in her lifetime.

ROYAL COPENHAGEN PLATES

Our marriage
hangs suspended
on the wall,
thin soft wire
carefully threaded
through the holes
in its fire-glazed
heart
precariously
balanced on needle
like nails hammered
into sheetrock conveniently
laid over
the messy scaffolding
of eleven years.
Blue
and white faces
of the Danish landscape
studied poses

of the cat
and the Christmas
rose, a hare
in winter, the owl
at midnight—
beguiling simplicity
of a world
lost.

CHASTISED

The child in me
always cowers
seeking a dark small closet
filled with softly
hanging clothes,
long-sleeved dresses
generously willing
to draw me within
their flat, thin
arms, permitting
my feverish
head to rest buried
between the folds
of an empty lap
quieting the throbbing
blood in my ears
the frenzied racing
of my heart until I
finally sink
down into the clutter
of shoes, an old
briefcase, the type-
writer, and listen
for footsteps. The

familiar fear: waiting
and wishing for discovery;
the longing for
oblivion.

Thomas Whitehead (1943–)

The consummate individualist, Thomas Whitehead spends his days writing poems and repairing bicycles, having, it seems, given up on greener pastures long ago—he now lives simply but contentedly on a modest cul-de-sac in Carson City. A founding member of the Ash Canyon Poets—and one of its most gifted—he writes funny, offbeat, "one-last-look-at-the-world" poems. His parodies on *New Yorker* poems are legend, and he can be seen carrying a green metal box filled with poetry books wherever he goes. His poems have appeared in *Beloit Poetry Journal*, *Interim*, *Bristlecone*, and others. Few people that are familiar with his poetry doubt that his poetic contribution will be significant.

AND ONCE I WAS IRISH, AT LEAST

There was no one with me, so
I took my hot baked potato
and while I ate the other
portions of my uncomplicated dinner,

held the potato inside my jacket
and right over my heart,
and you should know, before
we part, how I was better for it.

A LUNIST AND HIS LUNISM

May gold turn white through silver soon—
my moon is the daytime moon,
that one so seldom spoken of;
the pale, faint and faded, disappearing
into blue is the moon I love,

where the gentle knives of melon eaters carve
in the blue shadows of blue valleys
and along an ocean with an earth-borne tide.
There the unbordered kingdoms of daylight hide
from us and disappear by ancient magic
before the hard, intrusive glare of night.
My moon is obsidian soon, sings
a harmony of diminishment, turns
away behind the top-most trees
upon a distance new with morning.
It is all for love and nothing tragic
and will grow dull before a calculating
gaze without the slightest warning.

SING, COLUMNAR MUSE, OF ME THE LAST IN THIS BIN

Male ectomorph, extreme, 42,
hazel eyes; soul, light blue
(photo on request, please send
one of important part of you);

currently a well-established
failure in the absorbing concerns
of the dominant culture and
subdominant as well, possible
success in others; ruling-class
origins, downwardly mobile
background (since '29) have
little family, a few obscure
but otherwise charming friends;
unpublished writer, unshown
artist, unschooled teacher,
undiscouraged but unambitious
(expect substantial diminution
of civilization, loss of inventory,

leisure, next 1.000 years); value
unconstrained simplicity in all
things, have exquisite taste kept
well under control, not a sybarite,
treat money generously but firmly,
do not define self or others by
external circumstances; extremely
tactful but committed vegetarian;
handy with machinery, pen, shovel,
carpentry tools, rag and broom,
pleased to do mindless tasks for
good people with important work;
treat children as humans, loathe
cutesy poo and all random or
doctrinaire severity; no sociopathic
tendencies (references provided)
except the occasional and harmless

xplicxxi sox rex
rodx emptxnexx
humx xxyzox hx
thrux thx tulix

common to all, take a drink
once a week; allergic to tobacco,
most plastics, cheap thrills, expensive
fun, vulgar display; ex-savage
wit, largely cured of intellectual
nastiness, usually decline to
argue, occasional silent brooding
managed in Byronic style, never
petty; enjoy cultural pinnacles
without valuing them overmuch;
attempting hinayana-mahayana
synthesis but easily distracted;
enjoy cultivating a garden,
weeding fields of endeavor,
exchanging books and prophecies;

find most sports and travel silly at
best, have traveled widely in western
civilization, been frightened from
time to time, never bored; have been
through the political woods, keeping
a leaf or two from each tree, would
be a utopian socialist if possible;
find all competition ultimately
destructive; believe the human
capacity for self-delusion to be
infinite; cherish a circuitous
courtship of gentle purposefulness
and play; will modify facial hair
to suit, will improve currently
rusticating manners to the pitch
of current urban sophistication,
will change little else without good
reason developed carefully over time;

considered by very many to be
(this is just a caution) strange;
seek woman desiring househusband
all-rounder.

William Wilborn (1943–)

William Wilborn was born and raised in Missoula, Montana. He attended Stanford and later Cornell, where he received his Ph.D. in English. For over seventeen years, he painstakingly wrote and revised *Rooms*, his first book of poetry. Unlike many poets writing today, Wilborn has developed a voice that is rich in rhyme and meter—"a formalist" in his words. It is precisely because of his choice to write in (most frequently) the sonnet form, that it has been more than a little difficult to find literary acceptance, despite having been published widely in such periodicals as *Poetry*, *New Criterion*, *TriQuarterly*, *Yale Review*, and *Threepenny Review*. With time out for a Fulbright-sponsored trip to Finland, he has worked with many young writers over the years at the University of Nevada, Reno, where he teaches literature and creative writing.

Rooms. Omaha, Nebraska: Cummington Press, 1991.

GETTING IN THE WOOD

At Richard D'Abate's Place near Sanford, Maine

Having wasted my life too (as the poet said)
not noting butterflies especially
on the sweet plantations of a summer friend,
I sometimes wonder, Rich, how half
a dozen acres of mosquitoes, poison
oak, these graves of someone else's dead,
a house uninsulated and a shed
can benefit a man enough like me
(you from the fish-shaped suburban island,
I from the hub of five great western valleys)
to seem my double sometimes, more than kin.
Even the oak you buck and I retrieve,
pegging it into your unchickened co-op,
rings like backyard bamboo chimes

in Flushing or Missoula, Minnesota,
anywhere. I don't think prettiness,
fine fields of golden horse turds in the sun
or the sweet *far niente* of a hammock sling
could have brought you here to this penultimate
cold Thule of our corporation state.
I'd guess it was the need to know
how labor feels, the kind that keeps you warm,
and fear, beyond the city fear of men,
and love, and for a man like you (like me)
the thought about it later, all those words
sought and considered, saying *things have meaning*
more than what we suffer when we live.
You ride the chain saw and the stove-lengths fall,
and Mattie in the shed shouts at us Please
don't pitch them in the door so close to where
he's stacking. Never mind, you grumble, the kid's
been hit before—and men aren't boys in Maine,
you add, then glance involuntarily
at every stick I toss. (We being bourgeois
family men are careful of such things
as having one son only and one daughter.)
I think of Frost, the farmboy and the saw,
the pitiful hurt hand, the family
that will not go behind a preacher's talk
of glory and transfiguration
or of their own dull earth's imperative:
You've got to get the wood in to survive.
And that's true too, a country truth
that breaks suburban hearts like ours because
we've never had to live that way. But how's
a man like Frost to live? What's the good
of contemplation if it makes life harder,
even, for those we love, intolerable?
The burden's having words for love and fear
—not family words, more touch than utterance,
not preacher's words of dust and resurrection—
that can't be uttered in the living room

yet must be uttered if a man will live.
There are ways to warm a house, my friend,
with wood and words, and ways to chill it too.
—Did I say preaching? Rich, forgive this backyard
sermon of a man with nowhere to address
old habits of muttering wishes under his breath
pretending poetry when he means prayer:
May we steer clear of our temptations, pride
inverted in despair of recognition,
anger at those who cannot understand
our great need to be understood. Christ keep
us out of hammocks: make us realize
that if, in getting in the wood, we have
been overburdened with the word,
three times—in labor, fire, poetry—
we have been warmed. Our lives have not been wasted.

FOR AUNT LIZZIE

Where the town slopes away to the river
today wind shakes the weeds
where you lived, sitting by the window
waiting, while the summer sun
ran like a fever in the trees.

So many summers, up the long hot
staircase stinking of linoleum,
dark varnished doors, the transoms
gasping on their hinges, into the dry
still suffocation of your room.

On the courthouse lawn, over the trees,
at noon the Doughboy charges silently
forever the five and dime, and boys
lean bicycles in the dust and slurp
cold water welling from a China dome.

Auntie, it was light and air, water and earth:
when the sun went down you
watched it from your window, silently.
And we went on, as we must,
under the darkening trees and heard
the river's brassy artery on the lawns.

I never thought of you.

ON THE EDGE

Something about us, you maybe,
the sunk sun or the sinking star,
that rocky shelf above the sea
where wind combed in the summer grass,
that made me turn and nose the car
slow crunching to the precipice.

Maybe it was only me,
something I'd already seen
of sky and earth, the shadowy ledge,
the grey wash of the sea below,
two lovers in that place between
them and the letting go,
that moment at the moment's edge,
the sudden grace of gravity:

the long step taken finally
two people took once for their fate
so long ago, so willingly,
and so precipitate.

THE WEDGE

Too honest for a wedding ring
She cleaves unto her father's name
And husbands with a hyphening.
But what's a symbol if its meaning
Like a broken circle begs explaining?
Why so punctilious to mark
The cleft that sets two souls apart
When there's enough of world and time
To hyphenate a human heart?

Red Shuttleworth (1944–   )

Red Shuttleworth's poems and short stories have been appearing in journals like *Kansas Quarterly*, *New Mexico Humanities Review*, *Prairie Schooner*, and others since 1974. A Nebraskan at heart, he lived for years on a ranch outside of Winside in western Wayne County, Nebraska. A former ball player, much of his poetry and prose centers on baseball, the plains, and farming in the Midwest. In 1988 he entered the M.F.A. playwrighting program at the University of Nevada, Las Vegas, and he currently holds a Nevada State Council on the Arts Fellowship in Playwrighting. He has written fourteen chapbooks, and in 1985 *Living and Sinning for Them* won the Signpost Press Poetry Chapbook competition. Several of his plays have been performed throughout the United States, and in 1990 *The Children's Hair Turned White* debuted at the University of Nevada, Las Vegas. He's never too happy out of the sight of cow country, but for now the southern Nevada desert is home.

Coyotes with Wings. Prince George, British Columbia: Gorse Press, 1990.

Western Movie. Bellingham, Washington: Signpost Press, 1990.

Living and Sinning for Them. Bellingham, Washington: Signpost Press, 1986.

Bullpen Catcher and Friends. Richford, Vermont: Samisdat Press, 1985.

Over the Precipice. Oklahoma City, Oklahoma: Broncho Press, 1985.

THIS TOWN SURE TAKES THE RATTLE BOX

The line at the video counter has to pass by
a poster of a white bull, with a parachute
floating in a swimming pool in the foreground.
Maybe it's a film about a rodeo bull who's spent
a glorious motel weekend.

I once thought
to name my son Crazy Horse (we got a
daughter that time).

I'm in another line
with a cartload of groceries. I hear
a few women behind me, but I don't turn
as they talk about renting a Madonna movie.
Then I turn around because they smell good:
four hookers in town from Pahrump—
pulsing pale make-up, much too grim-visaged
for showgirls.

The redhead holds up
a copy of *Town and Country* and smirks at me,
"Honey, ya think I can make the cover of this here?"
The prettiest one has silver studs on a blouse
which only covers one shoulder and shows a
bit of nipple on one breast; she asks me
what I like.

Ponies, all-night-waitresses,
cattle out in Nebraska facing the Missouri River,
and hookers in line with ice cream and cigarettes.

"Sure," she says. "You a prudent type?"
Then she strokes a bare arm. And the girl
standing behind her says to no one,
"It's a tough road." A fourth girl,
let's call her Purple Camisole,
looks at the movie poster with the bull
and says, "The fucker looks rank,"
and right away I like her because
I like country girls.

THEY BURIED SONNY LISTON AT THE END OF A MCCARRAN AIRPORT RUNWAY IN LAS VEGAS

Nobody
          claimed
                    your body
                              Sonny
And how
              did you get that hypo
      "suicide" needle
in your back?

                    Ron Lyle
          another Denver heavyweight
is back in town
                        (security guard
at some casino)
                    but I haven't checked
to see if Ron wants to do roadwork
like we did at the Dunes golf course in '75

          Say
                    Sonny
I spotted
          (in front of the Tropicana)
          this girl in black lace 'n red leather shorts
waitin' hopin' 'n so forth
          for Ray "Boom Boom" Mancini

Sonny
          can you hear the roaring?

ON THE EDGE OF EQUILIBRIUM

Again morning sunlight through plastic sheets.
It's like visiting home: all that's left
is the lower third of the brick chimney
I built, afternoon heat breathing out of it.
Or the way blood and fur goes into an owl's belly.
This sunlight has the dullness of a week-old wound.
Last night it rained enough to fill nine coffee
cans in our farmhouse. Little flames
peered from the propane heater's window,
eyes smaller than apple seeds watched as we
touched each other. And morning
is forks and spoons, the way we climb
out of the four-legged tub into rusted sunlight.

Timothy Bellows (1945–   )

Born in New York City, Timothy Bellows received his M.F.A. from the University of Iowa. A songwriter and musician, he played in a blues/rock band, dabbled in marketing, and finally returned to poetry after picking up W. S. Merwin's *Opening the Hand*. His poems have appeared in *Wisconsin Review*, *Southwestern American Literature*, *Phoebe*, and other publications. He has worked with the Northern Nevada Writing Project and the Piñon Poetry Festival as a poet and teacher. He now lives in Sacramento.

THE CAR HUMS

I touch your wrist quite
by accident and a soft

thought spreads like
flooding into my chest—

at once—the way
a tune comes from

the radio and I
go with it—barely

able to stay to watch
your strange face your

nameless hair—you wash
up and down the lit center

inside my body where
I'm so small I pick up everything

and so
I touch your wrist

Bobbi Curry-Cartwright (1946–   )

Ms. Curry-Cartwright hails from Sharon, North Dakota. After much travel throughout the United States, she completed her M.A. at Western Washington University. For the past nine years she has taught English at Chaparral High School in Las Vegas. Prior to that, she taught in Minnesota and Washington State. Her poems have appeared in *Orphic Lute*, *Voices of the Magestic Sage*, *Write Connection*, and other publications. She, along with Joan Cutuly, is one of the few poets working in the public schools in southern Nevada. Her voice is at once comic, satirical, and oftentimes a poignant commentary on the "wishes, lies, and dreams" of a woman.

THE SERENADE OF THE LOOKING GLASS

If second chances were real
and I could steal back the days
that have grown gray as I have,
I'd not appeal crossroad resolutions
but accept their verdict as somewhat just;
it was my feet that stirred the dust along the path.

What pinches at my soul
are not the hours of decisions,
but the faded seconds when none were made
and puny trivialities left me mangled.

How I despair when I remember wasted time
in pubescent agonies, cursing
    empty Saturday nights,
    breasts that would never hint of cleavage,
    and cheerleaders with swinging blond hair.

How I shiver when I retravel decades,
regretting not the early decadence, but
        the friends for whom I never paused
        when they would stumble,
        a first golden love revisited, a dream dissolved
        in vanishing hairlines and a paunch,
        and wishes for what I couldn't have.

And now, at forty . . . something,
with thickened waist but breasts defying gravity,
if I could tap my heels three times for one more journey,
I would
        drink more wine,
        say yes more often,
        and tell my father I loved him.

And now, the road still stretches ahead,
and as the distant shadows beckon,
I nod and fill my glass.

CHOICES

I wish I really could believe
cigarettes are as bad as they say;
even though months have passed
since soothing smoke caressed my lungs
and curled around my head in wreath-like halos,
I would still prefer to give up instead
my first-born child (if I had one)
or my good reputation (if I had one)
or even my subscription to *Ms.* or *New Woman*.

THE REAL TRAGEDY

I chipped another nail today,
watched it lift,
          shalelike,
in much lighter layer
from the under-neath, and

knew I should find a clippers,
emery board/file
and trim it neatly,
all the while cursing the chalk
that stripped its strength;
but today it simply seemed
too much effort.

So I ripped it off,
leaving an angry whorl
all too familiar.

THE BEATING

Beneath her hurricane fury
he swayed, a slender sapling
helpless in the aisles;

Huddled between the Sparklets
          (and quarts of Pepsi)
he clutched the cart and
absorbed the battering
hail of bitterness
that never slowed,

Until she paused,
(a moment's lull for breath)
followed too quickly
by a lightning hand,
and another,
one strike after the other
that seared his cheek
and left him consumed.

ANOTHER SANTA ANA

Your hot silence blows through me,
and in its wake I am left dry,
an empty shell tossed
in the corner
by your currents.

Adrian C. Louis (1946–   )

Adrian Louis was born in Lovelock and raised in Wabuska, Nevada. After attending Brown University, where he received his M.A., he edited four tribal newspapers and is a founder of the Native American Press Association. Since 1984 he has taught English at the Oglala Lakota College on the Pine Ridge Indian Reservation in South Dakota, where he lives. His poems have been widely published in such periodicals as *Kenyon Review*, *The Texas Quarterly*, and *Contact II*. It is difficult to be unmoved when reading of life—his and others—on the reservation. The poems are passionate, vivid, and honest, but they do not shy away from their need to be written. He is an enrolled member of the Lovelock Paiute Indian Tribe and one of a handful of modern Native American poets from Nevada.

Among the Dog Eaters. Albuquerque, New Mexico: West End Press, forthcoming in 1992.

Fire Water World. Albuquerque, New Mexico: West End Press, 1989.

Sweets for the Dancing Bears. Marvin, South Dakota: Blue Cloud Quarterly Press, 1979.

Muted War Drums. Marvin, South Dakota: Blue Cloud Quarterly Press, 1977.

Indian Cheap Wine Seance. Providence, Rhode Island: Gray Flannel Press, 1974.

THE WAREHOUSE CHRONICLE

All morning I've stacked cartons of lipstick
on pallets pleased the liquor has steamed
away from my blood and breath.
Noon now in Rapid City and the studs among us
are out shirtless sunning diseased young flesh.
I sit on the cool, ancient floorboards
that have glabrous warps blackstained sad.
Christ, there's something unholy about muscled men
bullworking cosmetics when the scent
of their wives is still upon them

while their sweat-stung eyes embrace
the shimmer-gloss sluts on the cartons.
Hardly soft, these slurs of love whisper past
my pursing lips and prick my purple heart.
Minutes notch faster, slower, then faster
and democracy swirls in lessoning chaos.

Dear God these young men speak only of sex.
Their ludicrous boasts of great wet conquests
come easier than a whore in a rain barrel.
Raucous and clumsy they drop a new carton
then dancing in jest they lipstick their mouths
and I see, yes I see who they really must be—
great grandsons of Custer, his queer cavalry.

FALLON RODEO LONG TIME AGO

for Calvin Dixon

The bonfire laughed upward
flaming alternatives to innocence.
Nevada gravel whispered our ancient songs
under the boots of foreign Sioux cowboys
hand-crushing Coors cans
like the hearts of our brown-skin girls
who lanked around in sultry clumps
like the sweetest blooms of autumn sage.
Me and cousin Cal whose blood is full
sneaked up upon these funny Sioux
trying to snag out our girl cousins
in a corner of the rodeo ground.
Well, Cal yelled, "You Siouxs are homos."
Two big bastards ran after us.
We ran like batshit and hid in some bushes,
Cal and me, we were twelve that summer
and not part of the fire water world.

EPIPHANY: OXYMORON

In redneck God-fearing Gordon, Nebraska
verily comatose but parked upright
I think I thought I was
watching the rising sun wink and smile
but I squinted and groaned lacking simile.
The farmer streets were shyly human
in the absence of squaw-chasing sodbusters
who spit on redskins by daylight.
To commemorate the moment I unquipped my fly
and examined my urge to perceive sanity as something
more permanent than the early October
snow that was dusting my car.
It had been a hell of a root-tooter
the night before but two hours later
I was in class offering a quaint explanation
of the whiteness of Herman's big mammal.

The life of the mind is damaged goods,
I thought.
Too many trees have died for books
and I am trapped in this oxymoron
encased in concrete: An Indian college
run by white people in the name
of our bankable plight.

THE CHICKEN BLUES

Outside his room the rain
sizzles upon government roofs.
Inside, he fries chicken thighs
and tries not to spatter his unmade bed.
Whispers circuit through the smoke.
Tiny faces dance in the grease

and leap to his hand
to sink their teeth.
Faces of all the women who cooked for him.
He still lurks in the shadows of their eggshell skirts
and if he is fragile in his solitude
and scrambled beyond measures
of good, white taste
it is because of reasons
he has yet to manufacture.
He is the master of excuses.
He will quit drinking tomorrow
he has said for twenty years
but then again, maybe he won't.

INDIAN CEMETERY: LOVELOCK, NEVADA

for Steve Kane, cousin-brother

I'm at that place I grew up to leave.
Alkali-crusted sand waves have drifted
against my markers of blood: Grandmother,
Uncle Melvin, Uncle Adrian, Mom, my nameless
older brother born blue, and many others
I never knew and the many more I did.

Heyyy, this *Numa* girl has snagging eyes!
The few from my failing family
rake dead the weeds and arrange the incongruous
flowers beneath raging Nevada sun.
Strange unknown Indians with my mother's eyes
stare at me and whisper behind my back.
Their words unheard feel good and in my tribe's
burial ground I have no fear of death
and I have no fear of life
and in the silence of my people I light a Marlboro
and watch the desert sun wilt the white man's flowers.

This *Numa* girl has snagging eyes
and Grandfather, tonight
I will bury my old pain in her.

ennut: isn't it

NEAR EIGHTEENTH STREET

for Rosemary Joe

Them home boys at it again.
Helicopter spotlights dance upon Pico-Union
as bright as any movie spaceship landing.
Cholos with sleeked-back hair
are greased by cops against the wall
a story beneath your bedroom window.
Barely nudging the age-cracked shade
I peek, half-scared myself, at the alien scene.
It's one in the A.M. and the cheap stench
of tacos is still on the street.
Cantinas won't close for another hour
so I tiptoe to the fridge for canned solace
then hunker down at the foot of your bed.
We grew up together but never made love.
Squalor was the rabid dog that bit us.
I left the reservation and went to college
and learned that stream of consciousness was passé.
So I guess it does little good to count
the raging quips between sweet hips once held
accountable to my dry, Paiute lips.
Last week, some wild young L.A. Sioux
brainshot your sweet daughter dead.

SOMETHING ABOUT BEING AN INDIAN

There's something about being an Indian
we say to each other in a Bishop saloon
both of us forty with ponytails
grown down long to our Levi butts.
Yes, brother, it is the heart, and it is
the blood that we share.
The heart alone is not enough.

There's something about being an Indian
we say in soft whiskey voices that remember
many soft, brown women.
We laugh past the window and its vision
of constant traffic, the aimless yuppies
bound for the ski lodges.
Snow must be licentious for such fools:
white sheets to be soiled with temporal chill.
Yes, there's something about being an Indian
we say as we exit into the warmth
of Hell's secondary nature,
a place we call the Fire Water World.

THE FIRST OF THE MONTH

Undeodorized and radiant in rags
she squats sullenly
upon the crooked earth
and pokes her brown finger
at fat, red ants
dragging a dead fly home.
My reflection in her eyes
dazzles the air from my lungs.
I shrivel inside
the vacuum of formic arms.
Now's hourglass is frozen.

The bubbling brook is foetid
and the ancient, wondrous
songbirds are chancrous.
Against my dark void
of memories
of blood upon blood
White Clay, Nebraska explodes
with a thousand faces
of my drunken race
cashing their welfare checks.

Kirk Robertson (1946–   )

For over fifteen years, Kirk Robertson has operated Duck Down Press and, at one time, *Scree* magazine in Fallon, Nevada, with almost no money, very little help, and daily setbacks. Despite all of this, he has published some of the finest small-press books in the state during this time. He is the author of over fifteen books of poems; his *New and Selected Poems* has just been released from SUN/gemini Press. An accomplished visual artist, his work has been displayed in numerous exhibitions and museums throughout the West. Together with William Fox, he has been the mainstay of literary and avant-garde publishing in northern Nevada since the early 1970s. He makes his home in Fallon, Nevada.

Driving to Vegas: New and Selected Poems, 1969–87. Tucson, Arizona: SUN/gemini Press, 1989.

Matters of Equal Height. Reno, Nevada: West Coast Poetry Review Press, 1987.

West Nevada Waltz. Isla Vista, California: Turkey Press, 1981.

DRIVING TO VEGAS

Tonopah's
the only place
contour lines
appear
to rise

between there
and Goldfield
the first
joshua trees

beer at the Mozart Club

from then on
it's all downhill

between Mercury
and Indian Springs
the light
begins to change

you wonder
what you'll do
when you reach
the edge
of the map

out there
on the horizon

all that neon

beckoning you

in from the dark

HOPPER

an offwhite tempera afternoon
in a would be chrome diner

the sun attempts
to pour meaning
into what is best
seen at closing time:

last night
the slit ebony
cloth of the sky
revealed the cross
legged flesh of the moon

high heels hooked
on the rung of a stool
hanging on
in the trembling bar sign light

SCHWITTERS

Hearing the rain break up in syllables
—Pamela Stewart

early but never early enough
I come to shave the idea
of my face in the morning mirror

if only I knew where
everything is supposed to be
that is impossible

but something is near
I can hear the rain
breaking up in syllables

speaking slowly
trying out a new tongue
one nearly as fluid

as when love is new
things fall together like scraps
in a Schwitter's collage

of crumpled blue sky
I keep looking
out the window

wondering just where
you are right now
nothing is as innocent

or as unconnected
as we once
so naively thought

in the cabinet
six separate bottles
all saying *pain*

OUTSIDE ELY IN THE RAIN

bleary-eyed four a.m. cafe
your breath floating
in front of you

suddenly catches
the sound of a fan
back and forth

the crackles of red neon
push through the rain
across a damp gray field

stinking of sage

FOUR OR FIVE BEERS
DORSEY'S BAR
GABBS, NEVADA

Don't know why
I came out here

Circumstances
I guess

Weren't no woman
or the law

Probably
just cuz the wheel
didn't turn right

And you know
I've left
more'n a few times

But after a while
I start to feel like ice
must as it freezes
and I end up comin back

You know
I can't complain
if I get rained on

I know
it ain't no picture show

ALL DAY LONG

the air has been choked
thick with yellow dust
swirling like some angry
top around the basin

finally, late
in the afternoon
the clogged faucet clears,
the rain begins and

it looks like it's hailing
the manic yellow ochre
of a Van Gogh peeling
there in the afternoon

in between cloudbursts
sun struck wheatfield

ADJUSTING TO THE DESERT

It's been getting dark earlier
the light slipping away
before you notice winter
comes cruising up to the dock.

You wonder as you watch
the light fade just how
that ship you've been expecting
can come in here where even
the memories of the sea
have long since dried up
and blown away. Just then

three stools down the moon
crosses her legs high
lights a cigarette and

right at that moment
you know what it is
the coyotes keep asking for.

She leaves early after
driving everyone crazy
with the sound of her legs
drinking up their money
and making these promises
about how she'll show you
so much *more* tomorrow night.

You listen to the broken
hearted cowboys *just so lonesome*
they could cry while outside
the stiff October wind tears
at the petals of a neon rose
spinning everything in sight
like some nervous kid
his first time on a barstool.

After closing you stand
on the ditchbank and think
that by not expecting too much
or believing too strongly
in things that are either too much,
or not enough, here, and counting

only on the dizzy sense
of well being you get
under this totally
irrational sky

that, *shit*
you just might get by
after all

NOT QUITE DARK

and still over eighty

driving home
the twenty watt bulbs
of bathrooms adrift
in alfalfa begin
to throw their rays
of hope up into
the leaving indigo
and turning oh so quickly
to mars black sky
which now appears
to be running
right alongside
the car

your hand's out
the window
knitting feeble
white dots together
as it floats along
feeling the air
squeeze its flesh
like some not quite
ready
avocado

DRAWING TO AN INSIDE STRAIGHT

dust swirls behind you
down Indian Lakes road

almost there
you tell yourself

no longer sure why
you're going what
will happen

when you get there
fish and white pelicans

do you remember the time
your son slipped under
gagging spitting
as he broke the surface
glad to see the sky

the time you came
on a picnic

today there's nothing
only what the wind
left behind

muttering
in the trees

yeah, yeah
shut up and deal

Jean Boudreau (1947–   )

Born and raised in Fall River, Massachusetts, Jean Boudreau edited the University of Nevada, Las Vegas, literary magazine *Quicksilver* during 1989. Both a musician and songwriter, he played at Carnegie Hall when he was nineteen. He has been actively involved in community theater throughout the United States. In 1989, he received the Hiram Hunt Poetry Award from the English department at the University of Nevada, Las Vegas, for *Antelope Rising* (below), which is also the title of his chapbook. His poems have been widely published in *Interim*, *Hobnob*, *Gusto*, and *The Bugle*. Many people feel he is an important emerging voice in southern Nevada poetry.

Cravings I. Topanga, California: Triton Press, 1973.

DESERT WIND

cold comes to the South
West
where it is hot   dry
and lonesome
              for seasons.

where rock is red and oceans
are valleys,
except that the sand there
is not
       the beach. Yet the

       sky is blue
like anywhere else. People
like everywhere else,
       working the machinery

of the living. They build
            upon burning ground,
and hope
pours from every faucet. The

cold,
a lonely whisper
blowing throughout the night.

ANTELOPE RISING

The wanderer through October's song
begins
where there are only horizons. Yet
some journeys are impossible slopes,
embodied and blushed
            with deeds of belonging,

far
from the loneliness of muscle,
bone,
heart, spirit,

and whispered names. The wanderer
embarks
upon generous currents that
flow as underground wells
beneath the swallowed dirt,
and becomes part
antelope, part cry,
protruding and relaxed
                        between myth
and September's mist. There he crows

the melody of naked years
and stones that were once
warm faces. As man,
regret and perpetual loneliness are
the wanderer's view of rain. But
as antelope rising in the sun,
he feels the beast climb high

above the man.

Milly Brown (1947–   )

A student of Josephine Miles while at Berkeley, Milly Brown published many poems early in her career before, in her words, "real life" intervened. A Nevada resident for the last eight years, she was the literary advisor to *Autumn Leaves* and a former member of the Placerville Poets. After multiple careers she migrated to Reno where she now works for Washoe County. Her poems have appeared in *Kenyon Review*, *Green Flag* (an anthology edited by Lawrence Ferlinghetti), *Touch*, *Hiram Poetry Review*, and others. She is her own poet, one who has kept on despite the vagaries of staying alive.

DESPAIR 1

It is possible
that there are situations
for which there are no solutions,
that no amount of
assertive discussion
will make him more potent
or me more beautiful,
that there are things
like illness
and age
that cannot be avoided—
and death comes
too soon
and not soon enough.

OUR BROTHERS

They went to war.

He was nineteen,
sent to a psychedelic butterfly jungle
dosed with death.
He was a hero
in a surreal world,
while America watched The Fugitive
pursue the One-Armed Man.

He saw—and sometimes did—
unspeakable things,
which remain unspoken
except for weak, drunken moments
when they pour out of his wounds.
Then he can't forgive
his listener.

He came back alone to America,
a foreign country.
He is still alone.

Two marriages died for him.
He knows he killed them,
and he's not sure why.
He plants mines
in each relationship.
One can only walk carefully
for so long.

His work, if any,
seems absurd.
He spends evenings
in dope and drinking.
He doesn't believe in tomorrow
and hardly even today.

He forgets to eat.
A nurturing woman
feeds him,
loves him,
and lets him go
when her emptiness echoes
in a futureless space.

He wants to be a Casanova,
a rake, *roué,* or scoundrel.
He confuses
making love with fucking.
He has no love to make.

WAITING

Time is thick
sticky
the phone
deaf and mute
immovable
glued to the table
in a plastic trance.
The air is viscous
around the house,
the door gelled shut.
Minutes
jam together
and cling
to waiting.

BACK POCKETS

These men—
workingmen
mountain men—
manhandle machines,
manhandle women.

Sure they love,
but they keep their love
in back pockets
behind wrenches
and under rings of keys.

Truck driver,
hog farmer,
player of delicate guitar—
they are all the same.

They put their tools
where their tools don't fit.

Always at the edge,
never quite understanding
the pain they make,
they get hurt, too.

They carry their pain
like raw tattoos,
tender and blistered—
and they can't remember
why.

Jimi Sheryl Bufkin (1948–   )

Born in Fort Worth and raised in Tyler, Texas, Jimi Sheryl Bufkin worked as a security dispatcher, free-lance writer, and radio broadcaster while gathering material for her three chapbooks. Much of her poetry centers on a witty, heartfelt portrait of love in the 1980s. In 1990 she read in the Multicultural Arts Festival at the University of Nevada, Reno. While a student at Truckee Meadows Community College, she was co-editor of *Western Echo.* She lives in Reno and works as a PBX operator at a downtown casino.

Biggest Little City Blues. Reno, Nevada: Banner Printing, 1989.

Sometimes My Mind Wanders and Wonders. (Second Printing) Reno, Nevada: Tiffany Publishing, 1988.

THE SIDE EFFECTS OF "HOPE-TO-DIE BROTHERS"*

It wasn't an easy struggle . . .
A lilac spirit shining through a mahogany soul.
A child of the 60's blossoming into a lady of the 80's . . .
In search of myself I stumbled onto a woman,
Floating in and out of a fantasy world;
Mingling with the older crowd;
Magnetically attracted to younger men . . .
Those with dreams and a sense of humor still flowing through their
        groins . . .
Opposites sometimes . . .
With nothing in common except pride.

Brothers if we failed each other, could it be, I learned too late,
Small doses of your love are fatal?

*Poet's note. My definition of a "Hope-to-Die Brother": Any black man who can relate to any female regardless of ethnic background, but prefers the companionship of a black "sister" who has just as much ethnic pride as he.

Judy Carlisle (1948–   )

Judy Carlisle grew up in Wisconsin. After attending Marquette and Brigham Young University, she moved to Fallon, Nevada, where she lived for several years. A single parent and mother of seven children, poetry has truly been "an occupation of stolen time" for her. Along the way, she worked as a lifeguard, janitor, substitute teacher, bartender—at times three or four part-time jobs to support her family. Throughout all of this, she has managed to write honest—too honest for some—compelling poetry. In 1983, she read in the Piñon Poetry Series. Today, she lives in Carson City and works for the Department of Labor. She is a student of Byron and though her poems are riddled with the glamorless images of parenting and work, she continues to produce verses that strike the reader head-on. Her work has appeared in *The Meadows*, *Brushfire*, and *San Francisco Poetry Review*.

PLEA

it was—
apparently—
no problem.

parting the waters.

or healing the sick,
raising the dead.

all methodical,
every-other-day
miracles.

i have to be at work at one and
the laundry is a mile down the road at the laundromat—
wrinkling—
and the boys have baseball practice.
the first game is Saturday.

and this is
the FOURTH time.

Just asking, God—
Master of the Universe.
Do you fix cars?

A NEW VIEW

now I am old—
I live life in

smaller
spaces.

I no longer have energy,
nor time either,
for those marathon stretches of bald empty days spent in waiting

for appointments,
or acceptance,
or just the right conditions.

now I am old,
I don't believe in conditions.

There is not hope enough to risk
even one God-lit
sunrise—

or courage—
for more tears
than those of a single hour.

CEMETERY AT VIRGINIA CITY

The stones are broken now, and scattered over the sage-crusted earth.
Stones once laid lovingly in final remembrance of a hard-spent life.

Forty years,
Forty months,
Forty hours of existence in a damned and driven land.

In the Irish section—
(down and away, below the hill)
The same stories.
Priests, mothers, and miners—
Slaves to the search for silver—
Now to be had by pulling the handle of a slot machine in a saloon up the road.

How little we understand them.
We pass quickly, snap a picture and move on—
Leaving them to the remnants of their labor and their lives—
And the ghosts of their loves.

Passed over by the desert winds,
And guarded silently by God.

THE HEALER

Words, I thought, would heal.
Words of fury, pain, and passion dripping
down
the
page
like
blood
from a lethal cut.

Words to make you cry.
Words of a last, life-severing
Goodbye.

But my Byronic muse deserts me.
And in my bewildered brain are only muddles of mediocre
metaphors—
Whispers of once,
And long ago.

So I sit in silence, leaving the words to Shakespeare.

So I sit—

In silence.

And await the healing hand of death.

ON ENTERING MY FORTIETH YEAR

Halfway to the grave some say
(and I suppose it's true)
But now there is time.

Gone are the days of impassioned dreams—
And all that incessant striving—
Schools, marriage, diapers,
Divorce.

Now there is time—for me.

Forty years I've waited.

Why then,
At long last,
Do I count those coveted hours
Sitting at memory's open window,
Sobbing for the past?

ON FROGS

When I was in the tenth grade we dissected frogs.

I remember looking at them whole and healthy on a summer's day near the river—

Hearing them in the stillness of an August night through the open window of my room,
Lulling me to sleep . . .

And I remember too how eagerly we delved into them at school that fall—
Scalpels flashing—
Legs, heart, brain, body . . .

Down to the last muscle and sinew—
In search of

Science.

When we were through,
We knew all about frogs.

But down by the river,
The leaves and logs lay vacant.
And the nights passed

In Silence.

A DESPERATE THEORY ON THE MEANING OF LIFE

Somewhere under the dirty laundry,
Past the locked bathrooms that roar with the radio and smell of Max Factor—
Over the mound of molded plastic soldiers who died in the hall,
And on around the idiot box that beeps out the sound of dots like flies—

Is the little bottle that relieves my mental misery.

Today it was empty.
And I contemplated quitting until I remembered (while screaming into my pillow)
That buried between the dust bunnies and the despair,

Are the poems.

SEA STORY

When sailors talk of Navy days—
Of valiant camaraderie, and fierce fathoms—
Of exotic ports,
And almond eyed brown breasted girls who scent the nights with
perfume and speak to the music of coins passed under the table;

When they praise the sea bitch for her mastery of their souls,
and her protection from their passions—

No one speaks of broken hearts,
And broken homes.
No romantic rhyme about the wife betrayed—
In drink, or in loneliness—
And the desperate solitude that makes two betrayers of one.

There is no word for the child—
Standing at the water's edge gazing at a desert of sky, and sea—
Where a father's heart and hand should be.

THE EFFECTS OF THERAPY ON A MAD MOTHER

I used to hate the bad days.
The no good, nasty, rotten days when every injustice from
traffic police to social faux pas unjustly wreaked themselves on
my jumbled brain.

I used to scream at them, and wait.

Now—
In a structured cell of sanity,
Silent,
Except for the orderly countdown of the clock,

I'd exchange a thousand hours for just one bad day.

All of the answered aspirations for a single real
Regret.

Melanie Perish (1948–   )

Raised in Chicago but a New York City transplant at heart, Melanie Perish received her M.A. from Indiana University. She has worked as a poet in the schools, taught English in high school, and now works as director of corporate and foundation relations at the University of Nevada, Reno, Foundation. Her work has appeared in numerous literary magazines, including *Utah Holiday*, *13th Moon*, *Calyx*, and *Sinister Wisdom*. Her poems are the many voices of a woman working, writing, and fishing. All are bound to a female persona that lifts them quite remarkably to our ears, particularly when she gives a reading. Some of these poems are from her manuscript *Common Knowledge*. Most recently, she has teamed up with artist Chelsea Miller to exhibit an art/poetry show.

Traveling the Distance. Buffalo, New York: Rising Tide Press, 1982.

Notes of a Daughter from the Old Country. Pittsburgh, Pennsylvania: Motherroot Publications, 1978.

LINES

I write
short lines

thinking of all
the women

who write
short lines

before they wake
children

before they
scrape dishes

before they count out change
for the bus   thinking

wake
scrape

count out change
daily like breathbeat

then you are silver
in the early dark

YOUR MOTHER TAUGHT YOU HOW TO FISH

Your mother taught you

how to fish
but for supper
out of school
not for sport
kept you
to scout the deep pools

Your mother taught you

to break the forked branch near the house
to move slowly in soft shoes
near the creek bank   to keep your shadow
far from clear water   the sun
never behind you   never behind you

Your mother taught you

to use live bait
to crouch down be still
watch the fish
the flash   necessary
                    no pole
                    just line hook sinker
                    the brook trout
                    as simple words

Your mother taught you

the quick cast   no pole   the line spinning
the hook   in your service
the tug of bite   the fish mouth open
taking the live bait   and the stones   the stones remember

Your mother taught you

to pull   to pull
the fish
to hold the struggle
like words
                    not to play
                    there was no reel
                    the fish muscled and gasping
                    in your left hand

Your mother taught you

to reach into the mouth   find the hook
with fingers   slip it out
to slide the forked branch
to carry   to carry the catch home

Your mother taught you

on the bank
to pull in two movements
the fish
its fighting flesh

under the fir and tamarack
to respect the rainbowed scales
the fish   like words
would become your body

Your mother taught you how to fish

GRANDMOTHER

On the farm you watched me
let me help you feed the birds:
wrens and grosbeaks, a bluebird
like a flame against the gray-banked clouds.

We stood on the small porch
walked out back behind the kitchen
where suet hung in peach branches
near the lilacs you tended in spring.

You told me not to run or jump
not to go beyond the icy steps
without you.
I didn't listen.

In your old black coat, galoshes—me in
Gramp's jacket down to my red boots
we'd fling seeds and supper's bread crumbs
watch them pit the perfect snow.

In the spring we'd find birds—
one or two dead, frozen—still against new grass.
When you spaded your lilacs
you buried them and let me help.

When you went away
and Papa stopped saying you'd be home
when you became a window on the sixth floor
a pale hand in a plain white gown
when they found the stale breadcrusts
in your best Sunday bag

I sat on the steps and said nothing.

If you had stayed with me
I would have buried you
beneath the lilacs
with the birds.

STEEL

The locks of mill buildings, the peaked roofs,
the double row of dim windows
stand straight as a foreman;
the huge knuckles of pipe
fist their steam into the night.

The women know the yawn of the orange furnace,
the dead eyes of men in the lunch line.
The molten ore splashes,
seared with coke and flame,
unlike the flicker of votive candles
where they pray for the lost pension,
the supper stew, the safe birth.

The billets of steel thunder
and tough with tungsten
forge the beams, the scaffolds,
the huge coils of pipeline.
The women hear these
each in her own dreams.

From the slotted lights in the mountain houses
they watch the stars slip
beneath the river, the hazed moon,
the mill that looms across
the Allegheny bank—
the alloys of grief and will and silence.

SATURDAY MORNING

My mother washed the floor
on her hands and knees
and scrubbed the white tile shiny,
the bathtub, the toilet with a different sponge—
even after she became
the head of keypunch,
even after my father
worked regular hours in the union office,
and we could afford
help.

"People should learn to clean up
their own dirt," she would say.

Standing in the kitchen,
she ironed my father's shorts, small cotton slips.
Perspiration rimmed her breasts
in dark crescents
that pulled away when she bent over.
She swept the bread flour my brother spilled

into a metal dust pan,
crouched down
to wipe his hands with her clean hem,
to wipe the floor with a damp rag.

She was always
on her hands and knees.

FROM THE WHITE SINGLE WOMAN MIDDLE CLASS RECESSION BLUES: AN INVENTION IN PARTS

Today no men smiled at me
as I ran, as I paced past
the Museum of Natural History
along the park.

Maybe they did not like
my aging shorts, my baggy T-shirt.
Perhaps my ace bandage, the hair
plastered to my forehead offended them,
or the stick pin I carry in my left hand.

After all,
I was running against the wind,
running ahead
of Natural History.

REMEMBERING JOHN

Unlike other men who have grown
in my bed,
you reached for me in the night
out of a dream of orchards.

My palm on your rough chest
trunk turned toward you,
my arms strong and curved
and branching.

My mouth was early fruit you reached for,
when you held my shoulders,
held on
to keep yourself from falling.

ANNIVERSARY POEM: WEEDS

We pull weeds near the wood pile
pull through soil sandy with no seeds
pull near wood wet   with July.

After two years we work
together   bend backs   move the bucket
between us with words   without a word.

Our hands twist chickweed   thistle
we uproot again the ground with grip
and touch like the night we said

Let's buy this house.   Today
the hot sky stretches   the ground yields
to hands rough with love.

We leave clover   alfalfa
feed for things wild
while we pull near   pull through.

THE TROUT THAT DO NOT BITE

The trout that do not bite
nod beneath sandstone shelves
nap in dappled holes where the lake
drops. They sleep in pebbled coves
coves green as one-celled birth.

The trout that do not bite
nod   nap   in fresh water
float the loose ripples
twitch tailfins as they sleep.
The dream of sea-drag wakes them
the taste of salt downstream.

The trout that do not bite
remember they are not hungry   remember
the reason some call it   angling.
There are things you must not swallow
tho' they're red as Christmas
tho' they taste like *caviar*.

The trout that do not bite
have learned to wait   for rain
to feel the pelt of drops   the pock
of grasshopper   waterbug   beetle all
dropped to the light edge of water.

The trout that do not bite
have eaten their young and remember
death and life have separate hungers.
They choose to swim these currents
slowly   among their own kind.

William L. Fox (1949–   )

After receiving his B.A. in English from Claremont Men's College, Bill Fox moved to Reno, where he has lived since 1960. Shortly thereafter, he became the editor of *West Coast Poetry Review*, an avant-garde literary/art magazine, and founded West Coast Poetry Review Press in 1972. Over the years, he has published the work of poets such as George Hitchcock, John Haines, William Stafford, and others. The author of nine books, he experiments with form, style, and image to create his unique voice in poetry. For years he has been an avid trekker, having climbed or led climbs in Nepal three separate times. He has collaborated on several art/poetry books with visual artist Jim McCormick, and lately, has combined his publishing efforts with editor/poet Kirk Robertson of Duck Down Press. Due to the editorial work of Fox and Robertson, there is a literary record of small-press publishing in northern Nevada over the last fifteen years. He is the executive director of the Nevada State Council on the Arts.

Reliquaire, co-authored with Jim McCormick. Fallon, Nevada: Duck Down Press, 1988

Time by Distance. Fallon, Nevada: Duck Down Press, Windriver Series, 1985.

Monody. Woodinville, Washington: Laughing Bear Press, 1977.

POEM

old garden ladies
        are no benevolent force
they grow
        lean foods in their soil
        and have ageless teeth
they cast vegetable spells
and are immune to wasps
        they can tune the lawn
        to children and summon

wooden ships with wheels
        to sail away in
there is no speed in the universe
        like their hearts

KATHMANDU

white and simple
as a fence
        the peaks frame Kathmandu

pale and naive
our legs
        in long trousers

*

the cloth shops
all together
        a street hung
        inside out

*

when the bamboo scaffolds
are taken off
the temple
        just another pagoda

but for now
a jigsaw
of workmen

*

on the hill
looking down a line
of Hindu shrines
        one is a baboon!

*

at a corner
the pungency
of urine
has attracted
even you

*

nine at night
on the largest avenue
a policeman's harmonica
        heard two blocks away

*

next morning
a rooster appraises dawn
        we too have counted
        all night long

on the floor
our packs
tight as sleeves
rolled up to muscle

RAI FAMILY

strapped across his back
a dull tin wing

wife and children
each grasp a corner

every breeze
threatens divorce

he crabs sideways
up the trail
nose to the grinding wall

in the first monsoon
they'll all go mad
        under the new
        tin roof

YARSA

aspirin
she is as patient
with us
as with the flies
on her broken hand

downstream her mill
grinds bone with grain

DUDH KOSI

cold and opaque
the corpse of a snake
belly up
in the gorge

CHAURIKHARKA

too far ahead
i walk alone
thru the village

my back is a boulder
carved in mani

two women in a field
scratch for potatoes

mostly stones
they throw
over their shoulders

i sit on a rock
and wait for the cook

everyone follows
his basket of pots

*

and Lukla airstrip above
is on the lost plateau
        planes drop straight
        from Hollywood

        the icy peaks
        close up their circle

the old fuselage
on the runway
a dinosaur

KANETEGA

this is the wall
the wind hits
that makes the earth
go round

THYANGBOCHE

unsure if i
may walk thru
the gateway

a monk comes down
and offers wine

*

at the monastery
front stairs
are forbidden
but to the left
another door
where even Sherpas
must stoop

        a low doorway
        for humility

*

inside the temple
the faces of Buddha
peel off the wall
gay smiles
of curling paint

*

the courtyard
filled with firewood
no room for
dancing in the snow

*

the roofs held down
by stones
even so close
to heaven
        and still
        the monks
        have work to do

*

BREITENBACH

on the ridge
no room
for another grave

LOBUJE (16,000 FT.)

two hundred unnatural yaks
sit on your pack

all the way to Lobuje
the fragrant trail
of two hundred more

*

every now and then
the one breath
that keeps the lungs
from collapse

SHERPA WOMAN

braids solemnly
cross themselves
no no   we will not
undo ourselves

Jim Huskey (1949–)

Jim Huskey was born in Colorado and raised in Yerington, Nevada, and like Roger Smith, can attribute much of his interest in English and poetry to Jean Crawford, a rare teacher who shared more real knowledge with her students than most find in a lifetime of learning. He attended Harvard as an undergraduate, and returned home to found and edit A Frosty Morning Press. He has published widely in such periodicals as *Beacon Review*, *Bellowing Ark*, *Negative Capability*, and others. Along with Roger, he was instrumental in coordinating a "Poet as Humanist" conference in Reno, which featured Howard Nemerov among others. He now makes his home in Portland, Oregon.

Portfolio I: Poems. Fallon, Nevada: Sand Mountain Press, 1979.

THE HOUSE ON BUENA VISTA

I don't believe in accidental symbolism
Anymore. It is too cheap to draw truth
From the streets we live near,
Lying as we do between College
and Imperial. My view of the world
Is no better here than elsewhere.
A visionary, like a warrior, must work
At his task, must ready himself
For the invasion that may never come,
And standing beside the stone Buddha
In the garden guarantees no more
Than cold feet and damp hair.

FOR HOWARD NEMEROV, SUMMER 1979

Standing there among the blur and hum
Of the flashing neon lights, were you
As close to tears as we? You seemed
To want to linger, to shake my hand,
To hug my wife one more time.
Your poems had been fine things,
Like honest incandescent lights,
Like engine sounds and cello chords.
But in the end, poetry comes down
To this: a lonely old man and two
Lonely young people, standing
On a gaudy Reno street corner
Not really wanting to part just yet.

WHEN THE VEIN RUNS OUT

"Another?" Ben asked, pouring pitchered beer.
We'd climbed down throats of eight or nine old mines
That day, and we'd hunkered in a corner booth
To share a pizza, talk some poetry, ease
Our arms and feet. Behind us lights were coming on
And we, two beers to leeward, grew reflective.
Before us, street lamps wrestled with the dark.

I-80 splits Reno in half. Uphill
Old pines harbor the college where Ben works.
Buildings, some a hundred years old, still stand,
Built of bricks Eliot's father might have made.
Downtown, casinos glitter past dawn, parade
Their promised wealth for every two-bit tour.

Ben lit a cigarette and gently blew smoke
At the world. Born in Butte, he'd gone to Yale,
Came to Reno like some weed the winds
Of fortune had blown against a freeway fence.
At forty he felt caught, taught Yeats and Frost
To kids who neither knew their names nor cared.
In self-defense, he wrote poems, sifted through rock
On sites where glory holes had petered out.

Relaxed we speculated about the minds
Of editors, ruminated over Donne
And his newly acquired critical acclaim.
Ben stirred some ashes on a dish. I watched
The stoplight cycle twice. Ben's face grew still
As if he moved inside a pitch black room
And feared he'd break any lamp he brushed against.
He turned an ashtray with both hands and spoke
Like lonely thunder rumbling down a ravine.

"Remember Jerry Clark? I came across
A batch of poems he'd left with me last year."
I'd met him once at a wine and cheese affair.
He worked a graveyard Keno shift: small change
And no tips for the delicate Chinese marks
He made on paper. During the day he wrote
Philosophy and studied Greek. He knew
Four parts of *The Waste Land* by heart and read
The fifth each night he rode his bike to work.
Last June, as he walked his bike across Lakeside Drive,
A drunken Missouri tourist drove him down.

We paid our tab and walked past the bus stop.
I headed home. Ben crossed the street with the light
And started up the path that led to the library,
Returning books that were long overdue.

WAITING FOR TOMORROW

Oh, to be on a farm right now,
Standing in a field or woods or backyard
Garden patch, to feel my toes grip
And branch out into dark soil,
To feel nervous energy shoot out
From fingertips and hair ends,
Feel it bore into clean air
Like eager roots in the rain time,
To reach out with every inch of my skin
And sense the outside world
Reaching back with savage and gentle care.

For here in the city, my life is cut up
And parcelled out in surveyed lots
On asphalt streets. I imitate all
That surrounds me and wrap my arms
Around myself like swaddling bands.
Feet and knees hurt from pounding sidewalks,
Ears ache from screech and squeal,
And like an old coat too long in use
My nerves are frayed and tattered.
I cannot go on

Until I remember mowed hay and country rain.

BUILDING THE PUMPHOUSE

Crosscut saws, two-by-fours, three-penny nails,
Blue chalkline slapping plywood planks, what's true
And plumb and straight, my father taught me once.
He'd bought an acre—alkali, buck brush,
Salt grass—a lot to build a home on. I'd
Come back to find a summer job. Too smart
To handle tools, I'd grown apart, had learned

A tongue so strange, Dad feared we'd never talk
Again. Fighting for me the only way
He knew, he showed me how to use my hands.

I learned:

> The litany of carpentry: blisters, sweat,
> Handsaw's quick trochaic rhythms, Dad's voice
> Filled with the wheat fields and ballparks of his youth,
> The heat of nail after damn bloody bastard nail
> That bent halfway into Masonite sheets,
> Steel spikes that, hammered into pine, rose in pitch,
> Winds soughing in cattails and cottonwoods,
> How nights brought black thumbs, errant saw strokes, hands
> That failed, hammers that fell, mosquito blood,
> Hot showers, cold soda, long dreamless sleep.

September rushed upon us, wood unstained,
Roof half shingled, pipe, pump and water tank
Still undelivered. Sun had beat us down,
Rain had held us up. We might have rushed—
Painted the door, sealed drafts under the walls—
But as I boxed pants and packed books, I felt good
Knowing we'd finish the job another day.

Robert McGinty (1949–)

Born and raised in Reno, Robert McGinty attended the University of Nevada, Reno, where he received his B.A. in English. After studying in a master's program at UNR, he took a position at Elko High School, where he has taught English for the past fourteen years. Along with his colleague Kelly Moon, he has been a constant source of encouragement for young writers at this northeastern Nevada high school. He edits the *Elko County Writers' Festival*, an anthology of Elko County student writing. For a poet living in a boom-and-bust economy, one who reveres the environment, the area's fragile ecology holds more than passing concern.

ASSENT

Come, down from the high meadows
ringing the dry silt beds
of the old beaver ponds.
Come to the edge of the hanging
valley, then down
the switchbacks dizzy with wolfbane
and fleabane. Then yet farther
into the canyon where the creek
flumes in a rush of white
sound through twisted aspens
so thick you have to crawl sometimes—
and if you return
you know it won't be this way.
Come into the narrows where the only
gap is the water itself
numbing the stones, cutting down, pulling
your feet with the current, scraping
your ankles against stone, insistent
as gravity. Follow the shadows
that lead like a dark vein

always down until the sky closes
and the subterranean pulse is the single
sound, until the water becomes
wine and the stone wall
you leaned against is lost. Stand
in the depths. See the constellations
wavering on the water. The Great Bear
is your guide. The North Star—walk to him.
The only way up is down.

Emma Sepúlveda-Pulvirenti (1950–   )

Born in Argentina, Emma Sepúlveda moved to Santiago, Chile, at the age of seven. She had nearly completed a B.A. in Latin American history at the Universidad de Chile when Allende was overthrown in 1973. She fled Chile in fear of persecution and later completed her studies in the United States. Eventually she received her Ph.D. in twentieth-century Spanish poetry from the University of California, Davis. Understandably, her poems are filled with the anguish of war and the isolation of an exile. Like so many exiled poets, she has fought hard to remember the faces and events that made her love Chile and later leave it in fear for her life. She is an accomplished photographer and many of her photographs have been published in books or on covers of books by South American female poets. Currently she is working on an anthology of four Chilean poets and she teaches Spanish at the University of Nevada, Reno. This is the first time her work has been translated into English. (Translations by Shaun T. Griffin, 1989.)

A La Muerte y Otras Dudas (To Death and Other Doubts). Madrid: Ediciones Torremozas, 1991.
Tiempo Cómplice del Tiempo (Time Is the Accomplice of Time). Madrid: Ediciones Torremozas, 1989.

I CHOSE NOT TO DIE

For J.B.M. (1988)

They took me out of the coffin
and I chose not to die
raised me like Lazarus
surprised everyone with
a natural catalepsy
returned once more as I was then
the woman who did not believe in your mute hands
the woman who fled the sheets
every Sunday

for purification
behind the confessional box
the woman who at times
was an excuse
and nothing more
alone in the humid pillow
of adultery
the woman who dreamed she was lost
in your gilded eyes
to cheat death
and remain here
made living
made woman
forever
and not ashes
with the oily smell
of bones
demystified
forever stripped
of the human-animal love.

DECIDÍA NO MORIRME

A J.B.M. (1988)

Me sacaban del cajón
y yo decidía no morirme
me levantaba imitando a Lázaro
y los sorprendía a todos con
una catalepsia real
me volvía otra vez la de entonces
la que no creía en la mudez de tus manos
la que se escapaba de las sábanas
todos los domingos
para purificarse
detrás del confesionario
la que a veces

era una disculpa
y nada más que eso
sola en la almohada húmeda
del adulterio
la que soñaba perderse
en tus ojos dorados
para escaparse de la muerte
y quedarse aquí
hecha vida
hecha mujer
para siempre
y no cenizas
con el olor acietoso
de los huesos
dismitificados
alejados para siempre
del amor animal-humano.

HERE AM I NOW

for Ana María
Reno, Nevada, 1987

Here
am
I
now
Emma
laden
with
last names
with nothing from my past
a fine lot of nothing
waiting for them to answer
an exile who has endured much
and nothing cleanses
waiting for them to give me a certificate

that says I cannot go
and cannot return
until my bones decide
if it's here
or there
the place where the dead speak
and the crosses are silent.

AQUÍ ESTOY YO AHORA

Para Ana maría
Reno, Nevada, 1987

Aquí
estoy
yo
ahora
Emma
y
una
suerte
de
apellidos
sin nada de lo que traje
y bien poco de todo
esperando que me den respuesta
a un exilio que tanto dura
y nada borra
esperando que me den un certificado
que diga que no me voy
y que no vuelvo
hasta que los huesos decidan
si es aquí
o es allá
el lugar en donde las cruces callan
y son los muertos los que hablan.

YOU CANNOT LISTEN IN DEATH

You cannot listen in death
to the birth of noise
no one can hear
a single voice
nor a single word
that still tells us
life beckons
in death you cannot listen
nor hear
forever
the deaf chime
of the beats
in the heart that loves us.

In death, my companion,
you can only hear
the silences of time
that slowly separate
our bodies in ashes.

YA NO SE OYE EN LA MUERTE

Ya no se oye en la muerte
el despertar del ruido
no se escucha
ni una sola voz
ni una sola palabra
que diga que todavía
nos nombra la vida
en la muerte ya no se oye
ni se escucha
para siempre
el repiquetear sordo

de los latidos
de un corazón que nos ama.

En la muerte, compañero mío,
solamente se escuchan
los silencios del tiempo
que lentamente nos separa
en cenizas el cuerpo.

SEPTEMBER 11, 1973

Santiago, Chile

We will overcome!
I heard at eight
we will overcome!
I heard again
at nine

and at ten
and at eleven
and all
of the hours
of the petrified day

after

the voices

lowered

weakened

folded

and the silence

devoured the echo

echo
        echo
echo
        echo
echo
        echo

without me realizing
it became
the sound
of bullets
against the body
who rose in opposition.

11 DE SEPTIEMBRE DE 1973
Santiago, Chile

¡Venceremos!
escuché a las ocho
¡venceremos!
escuché otra vez
a las nueve

y a las diez
y a las once
y a todas
las horas
del petrificado día

después

las voces

bajaron

flaquearon

se doblegaron

y el silencio

devoró el eco

eco
    eco
eco
    eco
eco
    eco

que sin darme
cuenta se convirtió
en el sonido
de las balas
contra el cuerpo
de los vencidos.

THE LAST PRAYER OF SEPTEMBER

Santiago, Chile, 1973

Twisted on the floor
You compelled me to pray.
"Hallowed be thy name—"
Outside
the bullets were background music
to the cries
the cries followed the rhythm
of the bullets.
"Thy will be done—"
Bullets
and cries.

"As we forgive
our debtors—"
Just bullets.

....

....

I stopped praying.

....

....

My throat was clotted
and a lone tear
grew from the outside
toward the inside.
I absorbed it slowly
swallow by swallow
in body and spirit
made me drunk forever.
And never woke
not in night
not in day
not in the hour of this final abortion
when my fetus fires the last bullet at You.

EL ÚLTIMO REZO DE SEPTIEMBRE

Santiago, Chile, 1973

Retorcida en el suelo
me obligaste a rezar.
—Santificado sea tu nombre—
Afuera
las balas daban música de fondo

a los gritos
los gritos seguían el ritmo
de las balas.
—Hágase señor tu voluntad—
Balas
y gritos.
—Como nosotros perdonamos
a nuestros deudores—
Solamente balas.

....

....

Dejé de rezar.

....

....

Se me anudó la garganta
y sentí una lágrima
que crecía desde afuera
hacia adentro.
La absorbí lentamente
litro por litro
y en cuerpo y alma
me emborraché para siempre.
Para no despertar
ni de noche
ni de día
ni en la hora de este aborto final
cuando mi feto te dispare la última bala.

I GREW ACCUSTOMED

for Jenny

I grew accustomed
to fences within
did not speak
as the blood
gorged through veins
but did not run away
I was made strong
with muteness
that concealed me
long enough to think
and return to think
to give feeling
in this perpetual silence
I grew accustomed to being silent
drew dreams in memory
told stories
in the solitude of the mirror
made one voice
with darkness
I invented a proper world
with the hallucinations of breath
to drink in short sips
the threats of the time
and wait
wait until someone or something
tells me I am mute no longer.

ME HABÍA ACOSTUMBRADO

A Jenny

Es que me había acostumbrado
a no decirlo
a guardarlo adentro

como la sangre
que galopa por las venas
sin desbocarse
me había hecho fuerte
con esta mudez
que se esconde sola
me bastaba pensarlo
y volverlo a pensar
para darle sentido
a este silencio perpetuo
me había acostumbrado a callar
a dibujar sueños en la memoria
a contarme cuentos
en la soledad del espejo
a hacerme una
con la voz de la sombra
me había inventado un mundo propio
con los alucinógenos de la respiración
para beberme con sorbos cortos
las amenazas del tiempo
y esperar
esperar hasta que alguien o algo
me dijera que podía hablar.

nila northSun (1951–)

Born in Schurz, Nevada, and raised in the San Francisco Bay area, nila northSun received her B.A. in art from the University of Montana at Missoula. For years, she co-edited *Scree* with Kirk Robertson. Her poetry has appeared in Edward Field's anthology *A Geography of Poets*, *Vagabond*, *Turpentine on the Rocks* (a German anthology), and numerous Native American anthologies. A Shoshone Chippewa, she is the tribal social service director on the Fallon Paiute Shoshone Reservation, where she makes her home.

Small Bones, Little Eyes. Fallon, Nevada: Duck Down Press, 1979.

Coffee, Dust Devils and Old Rodeo Bulls. Canada: Opal Nations Press, 1978.

Diet Pepsi, Nacho Cheese. Fallon, Nevada: Duck Down Press, 1975.

LITTLE RED RIDING HOOD

laying in the hospital
after a heart attack
gramma called as many of
her eight sons she could find
she didn't call
her only daughter
babe age 34
gramma never knew where
she'd be
jail on the streets
in a bar in klamath falls
or shacking up with one of
her chicano or indian dyke lovers
in LA

babe left home at 16
married a regular capt. hook
complete with a patch over his eye
a damn good poker player but
she left him a year later

in & out of jail
car theft robbery
narcotics bad checks
she went from 120 to 180 lbs.
cut her long black hair into
short bleached chunks
got her face bitten & chewed
by her jealous girlfriend
started talking like a black pimp

gramma didn't call her
but she showed up at the hospital
a bottle of whiskey in one hand
a can of beer in the other
freshly beaten up
oozing cigarette burns on her arms
slobbering & crying
"momma, momma"
babe was the only one
who came to visit gramma

THE WAY & THE WAY THINGS ARE

gramma thinks about her grandchildren
they're losing the ways
don't know how to talk indian
don't understand me when
i ask for tobacco
don't know how to skin a rabbit

sad sad
they're losing the ways

but gramma
you told your daughters
marry white men
told them they would have
nicer houses
fancy cars
pretty clothes
could live in the city

gramma your daughters did
they couldn't speak indian anymore
how could we grandchildren learn
there are no rabbits to skin
in the city
we have no gramma there to
teach us the ways

you were still on the reservation
asking somebody anybody
please
get me tobacco

WAREHOUSE POEM

every preconceived notion
of what a warehouse job involved
was true
and then some

day 1
job interview
i pulled up in the parking lot

just when they were taking a break
what poured out of the doors
scared me
looked like convicts to me
tough & mean-looking women
a few big men
a few big women
i knew somebody at the place
& had their recommendation
so i was hired
wear closed-toed shoes
was all they said

on monday i wore corduroys
a nice sweater &
high-heeled boots
they sniggered when i walked by
i never sat all day just walked
concrete floors
those boots never saw that
warehouse again

day 3
i never heard such dirty mouths
not since college anyway
they referred to each other
as bitch & tramp & airhead
& gossiped & manufactured rumors
& accused anybody that seemed to get
a break as having blown the supervisor

a week later
yes there are some
bitches & tramps
i found myself saying
"what a bitch she is"

2 weeks later
some alliances form
jokes are told
cliques start forming
them & us
the pickers
the packers
the checkers
the stockers
the supervisors
we don't hardly see the office staff
they're the ones in heels and dresses
we're in dirty nikes, worn out jeans
& t-shirts with writing on them

a month later
we work next to each other
8-10-12 hours a day
6 days a week
we talk about boyfriends
husbands
a lot about ex-husbands
what they got in the divorce
what we left behind
the jobs we had before
another warehouse
cocktail waitresses
part-time students
most fairly young
still have big plans
for the future
lab techs
counselors
go back to school
put a down payment on
a trailer
put money in the bank so
she can kick the boyfriend out

3 months later
we talk about sex
we say things we never told
anybody else
we spill our guts
& learn new things

5 months later
we comfort each other
within each clique
& get to know some
of the others
they're not so bad
& the bitches you just avoid
their 'friends' are the new
employees that don't know better
we say soothing things to
the ones that need a good cry
& we all do sometime
the work is hard
the bosses unsympathetic
the families neglected
guilt, depression, exhaustion
the paychecks come & go
we don't see the blue sky
our skin is too white
they grumble about our
bad attitude
some are fired

8 months later
a couple handfuls of
the "original" crew are still here
even some of the bosses
& supervisors are gone
a lot of new faces
we barely bother to
get to know

everybody seems to have
job applications out
rarely a job interview
we've gotten raises
plus the overtime pay
it's hard for other places
to come up with the same amount
the idea of a cut in pay
& starting over
is not attractive
and hey
except for exhaustion
we're in muscle-y good shape
lost weight
firm underarms and thighs
but who knows but us who seem
now to live here
too tired to go out & party
though a few manage
& are laughable zombies on
the saturdays we work
we keep aspirins & pepto bismol
on hand

11 months
then the call or letter comes
you've been hired
or sometimes the call from within
the warehouse
you've been fired
& whichever the case
you can feel the chains
& the yoke fall off as
you open the door
& see blue sky & feel fresh air
you're free.

Robin Elizabeth Davis (1953–   )

Born and raised in Lithia Springs, Georgia, Robin Elizabeth Davis moved to Nevada in the late 1960s. A natural-childbirth educator by training, she lectured at the University of Nevada Medical School for several years. Her poetry is wrought with images of birth and loss, yet it is musical, fervent, and direct in style and tone. These poems are born of much more than a love of words—rather, a love of a living language, one that names the essence of being a woman. They have appeared in *Interim*, *Southwestern American Literary Journal*, and others. Her first manuscript, *Visible Light*, was completed in 1989. She is married to a doctor in the air force and they are currently stationed in Spain.

REQUIEM

He returns
the meadowlark father
suddenly in Summer
an abbreviated song.
We remember him in courtship
trilling arpeggio tenor against Winter

Now staccato notes of August
announce nestlings alive—
a natural argument toward
soaring red-tail hawks above—
his chartreuse vest a startling presence
sentinel over dry field grass

And the waiting flowers I love.
What are we doing here—
higher animals—jealous always
where law provides. The winged female
close to the empty earth
wears in every season, lesser plumage.

Redemption in these short clear notes
these simple fine assumptions—
those who have done the good work
which species preservation demands—
stand the rotting fence in wild color
singing on any evening
directly into the wind.

NOW HER SMALL GRAVE

these branches lie broad
now eleven years wide
where shade has grown

piñon—some translation
of shadow and longing
where below you lie

in your quilted grave—natural
predators in barren seasons
where daily the dark dreams grew

never found you—never turned to
carrion the simple napkin of notes above you
where your fine fingers

warn the living away—never
ate from you or howled the find
where this frame of air fills

long hills with certain prayer around—
are the needles laughing now
where you still the brown surround

as they shimmer chiaroscuro
through cracks in fretted slate
where sudden gardens of garnet and

peridot grow your hill
this perfect flannel
where jutting here and there

rooted to some inner bearing or
defined in relief by useful bones
you lie in your small grave.

NOT FAR FROM OUR TOWN

1.

Not far from our town
hidden in a white buckle painted farmhouse
lived a tall grown boy
who would never leave home
with his soft white arms
that flailed in fits. His
Mama would own all his desires
for all his days
and when dark fell
the evening calling
        whippoorwill . . . whippoorwill . . .
he stood shy between matching posted beds
while her gnarled fingers
gave comfort to confusion
that sometimes wakes all boys
into the hard morning
of their wandering dreams.

LISTS THAT FOLLOW

I.

Buy sole for Friday—don't think
of last Friday when you did not know
don't think of the breast that is left

> (Begin removal of the breast medially proceeding
> including the pectoral fascia and intercostal perforating
> branches of the internal mammary artery)

II.

Calm the baby never near your heartbeat eating
close the last window—scream—again

> (With the breast now only attached at the axilla
> carefully dissect all lymph nodes—all fat—
> all breast tissue—leave blood flow and nerve supply
> fully intact to remaining tissue)

III.

Turn in overdue library books—pick up the right-sided child
adjust your sweater—someone is watching—they all are

> (Remove breast in block to prepared sterile field
> deliver to pathologist for gross examination)

IV.

Cook something for them between six and seven
excuse yourself pleasantly—throw up—again

(Using towel clips pull the skin flaps together
place a soft penrose or sump drain in the incision)

v.

Remember how you came to him face forward
cry for him—handsome boy—where do his hands belong

(Approximate skin edges with vicryl subticular continuous
sutures—strive for an excellent cosmetic result)

vi.

Sleep without nightmare one night tonight
wake clinging to your own sweat as the moon rises
change your nightgown—pray for an eclipse of all light

(Estimate blood loss—chart findings—thank crew
weep in lounge—recompose—hold her husband
pray forgetting—smile when she wakes)

Shaun T. Griffin (1953–   )

As the editor of this anthology, Shaun Griffin has become increasingly wary of "final judgments" with respect to poetry. Nonetheless, as he reads Nevada poets he is reminded over and over of the need to record "direct statements of acutely perceived experience," to quote a friend. This poem is offered as a symbol of this editor's kinship to all Nevada poets, both those who are here and those who are not.

Words I Lost at Birth. Fallon, Nevada: A Frosty Morning Press, 1981.

Believe I Don't Know Why. Yerington, Nevada: Mason Valley Publishing, 1979.

A PLACE OF STONE

I come for the wooded dance of the Comstock:
the piñon pine, harsh as the face of an owl,
juniper, a scruff beard on the high desert,
and locust, spent, with the purr of cicadas.

I come alone, in a blue-black forest of night,
steal my way into the folds of darkness,
risk ruin under the light of a star. I come
as so many others must, for that which is missing
from the stencil of the city: the outline of a face
on the back of a horse, the quiet rocks
that grow and grow in the sun's burnt strokes,
and the pine nuts glazed with sap in fall.

I come for the fissures that ripple through this land:
the empty spell of a mine shaft, water
dripping in like a slow clock from above;
the breaking, the chipping, the bloody salt smells
that ride the canyons. A trail of ashen dreams
flake the golden skin of Nevada.

I come to fill the fallow contours of my mind
with a place of stone, yet nearly everything
has been stripped from these slopes.
Even the cornflowers cower in the tailings.
Cattle graze on winter roots and a farmer
fingers heat from the stove.
Fences crawl over half-bleached plains,
touch the moon's corrosive light

and I return, a wisp of desert wood.

Gary Short (1953–   )

Born in Berkeley and raised in northern California, Gary Short came to Nevada in 1977. He taught English at Wells and Virginia City high schools and has worked as a poet in residence in several rural communities in Nevada. After leaving Virginia City, he traveled widely in South America. He returned to study with Dennis Schmitz at Sacramento State, and recently finished his M.F.A. at Arizona State University, where he served as poetry editor for *Hayden's Ferry Review*. His poems have appeared in several magazines, including *Poetry East*, *Chariton Review*, and *Permafrost*. Few poets have woven the people and landscape of Nevada into their work like Gary Short. He was a 1990–91 fellow at the Fine Arts Work Center in Provincetown, Massachusetts.

Looking Past Today. Fallon, Nevada: Duck Down Press, 1983.

TOWARD MORNING (PANACA, NEVADA)

The sky sleek as the coat of a blue roan
in the moon-quiet light of two thousand stars
falling on Fourth Street in Panaca.
The smell of dust in October air.
A horse whinnies, dreams she is part wind.
On highway 319 a hay truck shifts toward Cedar City

and the hours grow huge.
You don't know a town until you feel it silent
and walk to its end
past unlit windows. I remember Basho,
    Deep autumn,
        my neighbors,
            how do they live?—

The high school basketball coach
dreaming a six-foot-five transfer student;
the county road supervisor, his stubbled face
creased by the white sheet;
the short-order cook at the Silver Cafe
asleep with the smell of onions on her hands.

NEAR MINA

for Roger Smith

For now
this is all there is—
sky, sand and sun.

We travel on a road
unfolding its reverie
through small towns.

Thirty miles from
a quiet place,
a rundown bar,

a sign
with a faded letter C
advertising OLD BEER.

On the outskirts of town,
a crop
of abandoned cars.

In the distance clouds
lower long ladders
of rain.

Soon damp earth
and sage
will perfume the air.

200 miles
to Las Vegas,
and the hours

huddle together
like cattle seeking solace
from the rain.

FARNES EGBERT: WATER DOWSER

A forked cottonwood stick
defeats logic, points to water.
They say he's lucky.

Where dry land was, now
cattle drink and ninety acres
of hay nod in the wind.

He scoops a fist of dirt,
squeezes, lets the dust
stream silver from his fingers.

Today, south of Jackpot,
at the Winecup Ranch,
he holds the wings of the V

palms up, thumbs back,
and paces the desert, waiting
for the stick to pull

down. One thousand feet
below the water pulses,
tracing the veins within him.

TEST

You people who live near Nevada Test Site are in a very real sense active participants in the nation's atomic test program.
—Atomic Energy Booklet, p. 2, March, 1957.

The sky brightens in a flash.

A rancher feels the earth shudder
beneath his red roan.
He shields his eyes—
flesh is transparent,
his hand a diagram of bones.
My God, he whispers.

The mare shies,
only the pressure of his boots
urges her
through Eagle Valley to a ridge where
the only boundary
is the sky.

In the sparse shade of a Joshua tree
the pink clouds hover
over the ranges of his retina.

He rubs his burning nostrils,
tries to spit out the bitterness

the metallic taste.

JOHN W. MACKAY
(1831–1902), Miner

In my lifetime I was worth seventy million dollars,
that doesn't do me any good now. I was born dirt poor
in Ireland, didn't have one silver dollar
when I hiked over the Sierra to Virginia City.
I never drank to excess, didn't play
games of chance. As a miner I had outlet enough
for my hunches. Deep in the earth I chased
a knife edge seam of silver through the darkness
for weeks. Finally, it opened to the Big Bonanza—
an underground trail of wealth that we worked
feverishly for five years at $800,000 per month.
I tried to give my wife the world on
a silver platter.
I bought her mansions in Paris, London,
and Long Island.
I distributed silver to the poor and good causes.
A friend or favor was never forgotten.
You will have to search in order to find
anyone speaking ill of John Mackay.
My wealth was unlimited,
but my days on earth were not—
they flew past like a V of geese
headed south for the holidays.

TWO POEMS ABOUT WELLS, NEVADA

1) A Poem Overheard in K.G.'s Bar

This is the only town I know
where you can stand up to your ass in snow

and still
have dust blow in your eye

2) A Poem Blown Away by the Wind

THE CAVE BEHIND THE MORMON CHURCH IN PANACA

Not much deeper than the bed of a long pickup,
the bad boys come here
after shooting sparrows out at the sewer pond
to swap stories and carve petroglyphs
and names—theirs and others—in damp limestone.
A scattering of caffeine-free Pepsi cans.
Charlotte Larsen Is Pretty someone wrote,
so taken he had to tell it, if only to stone.
Most of the names scratched here
are listed in the slender phone book; they remain
as teachers, hay balers,
mothers, store clerks, and unemployed.
A few of the named are effaced
forever, gone in a truck
flipped off the road—teenagers trying too hard
to break the boredom between here and Las Vegas,
too fast, finding a darker place than this cave.

IF THE KENNECOTT SMELTER IN MCGILL CLOSES

Holes in the toes of the shoes
of that gap-toothed boy scudding
in the dirt at Copper Park
will grow ragged. Reaching for
the Nevada sky the smokestacks
shadowing the new LDS Church
will be monuments to the non-working man.

For Sale signs will bloom on front lawns.
The billboard on the edge of town,
its *Welcome to McGill—Copper Capital*,
will fade and peel above
the highway sign that says *End Scenic Route*.

When the afternoon wind rises,
the pulley holding no flag will ring hollow
against the metal pole in the park.
Punctual as the lunch whistle
used to be, men wearing baseball hats will walk past
the padlocked gates of the smelter.
Spitting their Skoal on the pavement
in front of the church, they'll go by
the boarded-up showhouse,
lower their heads past Bradley's market.

In the smokey gloom of the McGill Club
they drink drafts and between one beer
and the next, talk about what to do
when the unemployment runs out—maybe chase a job
to Elko or work as a roughneck on a drilling rig
with a brother-in-law in Wyoming.
It's a free country, anyone
can choose where to fail.

Some of the men, not wanting to go home
to meatloaf stuffed with soda crackers
or a son asking when he can have a bicycle,
stay at the bar and roll dice to see who feeds coins
to the jukebox that plays old Glenn Miller—
"In the Mood," "Make Believe," or "Am I Blue?"
If the phone rings, the bartender knows his line,
He just left a minute ago. Outside
the moon above the smokestacks looks on
pale and worrisome as the wives of McGill.

Roger Smith (1953–   )

Born in Billings, Montana, Roger Smith studied with Jean Crawford while he was a student at Yerington High School. After completing an M.A. at the University of Nevada, Reno, he finished his Ph.D. in English at Stanford University. He has taught at several universities, and during his many years in the Reno area he coordinated several poetry events including The Poet as Humanist series (with Jim Huskey), and the Blue Mail Box Poetry Reading series, held across the street from the university in the old Center for Religion and Life building. During this time, he and Gary Short edited the *Nevada Poet* anthology of 1981. His poems have appeared in *Brushfire* and other literary magazines. He now lives and teaches in the Portland area.

FINAL RECOLLECTIONS

Father, the wind goes out of you and you weep
to tell us what the doctor said:
the tumor deep in you insinuating.
And we who thought to diagnose
your constant recollections
of boyhood, Depression, Pacific Theatre,
and your own father coughing foam and blood
to be a kind of drunkenness
are your helpless children once again.
How intemperate and silly we
ourselves were to have tried
to interrupt your stories and fix you
more distinctly in our here-and-now.
Had we known how ill you were
we wouldn't have tried to save you
from yourself. Now you cough
and double over in your familiar chair.

We run ahead, you all but lost in our care for you,
to that long day when we'll lament
ourselves, and you'll recall us all.

Gailmarie Pahmeier (1957–   )

Raised in St. Louis, Gailmarie Pahmeier received her M.F.A. at the University of Arkansas at Fayetteville, where she studied under Miller Williams and John Clellon Holmes. In 1985 she received the Paul Laurence Dunbar Memorial Poetry Prize, and she is the first recipient of the Nevada State Council on the Arts Literary Fellowship (1988). She is currently writing a series of stories and poems on sports and teaches English at the University of Nevada, Reno. Her poems have appeared in *Interim*, *Tar River Poetry Review*, and *The Redneck Review of Literature*. Unlike many female poets writing today, her work has a desperate sensual quality that is unmistakably hers, and at a reading she is truly a poet come alive.

With Respect for Distance. Reno, Nevada: Black Rock Press, Rainshadow Editions, 1991.

OUT WALKING

This is one of those things I require,
a walk through night after common day.
It's easy to measure step, listen to the pattern
of someone else's feet several houses behind.
I'm unafraid; the dark is always deeper
farther on, waiting to take my legs.
Sounds out here are simple—the burn
of leaf against leaf, the battering
of bugs into light.
There's safety in these streets.
Somewhere in this neighborhood,
a woman cries into her man's thickness.
He lies there silent, thinking
if he could choose, he'd go.

LETTER TO AN ABSENT LOVER

You remember the false walls here.
This morning, about four, the couple next door
went at it their own way.
I sat up in bed, tucked the blanket between
my legs, smoked cigarettes, listened.

He had been waiting for hours, pacing,
turning the bathroom water off and on.
The lazy one-two sound of his boots
on the linoleum still lingers.
It is hard to wait for the clinking of keys.

She came home, called him a Southern son of a bitch.
His response, unclear, came clumsily.
After an hour and a half of slamming doors,
shattering things, and screaming, it was quiet.
Sometimes the silence around here is earned.

WITH RESPECT FOR DISTANCE

Before I pull into the parking lot,
I see him standing there, shirt-sleeved, pipe in hand.
Since last week he hasn't changed,
perhaps he looks a little tired.
His slow smile and I know I'm on time.

How's she runnin'?
The certain first question, his greeting.
I give the shrug, tap the hood of my car.
There is something miraculous about this machine,
how it has come to cement a father and daughter
separated by everything but this link.

We pass the day calling trucks—
Peterbilt, *Kenworth*, *Mack*.
Small words, none as striking
as the glint of chrome beneath his determined touch.
When I leave I know he is watching me,
waiting for the sound of malfunction.

What will I tell my children when he is gone?
He was a quiet man who could make things run.

NEIGHBORS

The typist who lives above him
tells him always she loves her work.
Once over wine she told him how cool
her fingers feel cradled in the hollows
of the keys, how the busy clacking reminds
her of a toy train her brother had,
then a real train carrying passengers
to mysterious places, like Montana.
She says, sometimes the letters as they
become words are like people running
to form a line for a movie or free food.
Even the quiet buzzing between pages
soothes her, for it is the purring of cats
that might escape all fateful drownings.
He likes this woman; she's a good neighbor.
Often in the evenings he sits to write
usually a letter to his lover
asking in another way: *Shannon, come home*.
He sets the stroke for heavy, beating down
so the sound will carry to the typist.
He imagines she's just washed her hair,
hears his plea rising through the heat vents,
pillows herself on the floor.
Her hair dries slowly as she eases into sleep.

THE SWING

The yellow metal seat flashes
in the casual sun.
His four daughters, all under twelve
and desperate to be pushed,
circle around him
as he waters the garden.

Swing *me,* Daddy!   Swing *me*!

You'd shoot the hose at us.
The water was hard and cold—right for August—
but there was a sudden tilt to your laughter.
The neighbor paused to watch your girls
running, bare feet springing the dandelions,
skin sparkling and dripping.

When I pass the park at night now,
I imagine a father swinging his daughter,
pushing her higher, higher.
The park echoes long trailing screams of pleasure,
as thick familiar hands propel her small body,
her skirt opening to gather the dark.

Kelly Moon (1959–)

Kelly Moon grew up in southern Utah and later went to college at Southern Utah State where she received a B.A. in English. She worked as a ski-lift operator and mixed automotive paint at a hardware store before starting work as a teacher. For the past seven years she has taught English and theatre arts, and has directed three student plays per year at Elko High School. In her teaching, she works daily to remind students that poetry is a living art form. Her poetry has appeared in *Tailwind* and other publications. When she isn't teaching or writing, she spends her time skiing and reading. She makes her home in Elko.

INDEPENDENCE

You didn't understand when I held
the broken guitar like a dead child

in my arms. You could not see
that it could never be repaired

or replaced or mine again.
The veneer face peels like

dead skin and the braces,
ribs of starvation.

The strings snap in my fingers.
The sound rings in my ears.

I rock back and forth,
sing a lullaby, one written long ago,

maybe not at all, one that originates
in the blackness of the stomach,

moves up the throat, into the mouth
and evaporates into the light.

THE STEPFATHER

I remember the time
he thought me a whore because
my neckline was too low.
He took his hunting knife,
split my blouse down the front,
like gutting a deer,
exposing fourteen year old
breasts in front of friends.
He laughed and squeezed and poked
me with his large rough hand.
I cried, would not leave my room.

Mother never knew.
She quietly made food,
cleaned, and opened her legs
to her husband like a good
wife should. He is dead now.
I should forgive him, but the scar
above my right brow, a crescent
shape still tries to blend
into the corner of my eye.

FISHING LESSON

To show me how to hook
a fish, you carefully climbed

into the dark pool of water.
Floating silently, you became the fish.

From beneath the surface,
you moved under the caddis fly

that floated on the top.
I could see your face emerge,

your lips circled the fly,
you mouthed it like a lover.

The fly moved in and out your mouth.
At that instant, I forgot it was you,

but thought of the great fish
of Hemingway and Melville.

I jerked the line to set the hook.
It embedded itself in the roof

of your mouth behind your
left incisor. I felt the barb

in the nerve, the hard lump
of skin you must have felt.

You did not struggle.
I did not reel you in.

You submerged, then floated.
In a flash of silver,

the current moved you down
stream. I let go my bamboo rod,

watched you both disappear.
I stood on the bank

holding my mouth with both hands.

L. A. Fleming (1962–   )

A native of Cañon City, Colorado, L. A. Fleming moved to Nevada in 1988. She is one of several new voices to emerge from the Ash Canyon Poets. A former editor of *Colorado North Review* at the University of Northern Colorado, she went on to receive an M.A. from Kansas State, and later won the Best of Book prize for her poem in *Caperock*. Her poems have appeared in *The Comstock Quarterly* and *River City Magazine*. She is currently a journalist living in Carson City.

THE RUBDOWN

we notice
the strong back
of a man, mineral
oil as it slides
under palms,
candlelight
smoothing skin
as much as darkness,

pressure
moves with us
from the inside
shoulder muscles
to neck
to the blades
to ribs
to spleen
to kidney,
the sides of his
body, back
up the spine,
the shoulders

again, knead
again, we notice

his man-scent
of evening,
the skin
of this man: and
under outstretched
wrists of our
woman's arms,
we knowingly
mold him,
we carefully
shape his rest,
we lovingly
slide him into
our own dreams.

MAP

There was a map of Vietnam
above the television set, and mother
said it's a war all right. We
watched it over dinner, keeping
track of it all as best we could.
Then as Dad read
the evening paper he'd say
long day. It's been a long day.
We'd wash all the ordinary things
after supper, put away the potatoes
and extra pork chops. Robert
would snap at me with a dish towel
so I'd cry and he could get away.
Mother made him stay. You
do your duty, she said.
No matter what. You were raised

that way and don't forget.
Later, during cop shows
and homework and more dessert
we would listen to Dad snore
in his chair. Mother held on
to his hand. He's a good man,
she said. Your father.

When he couldn't breathe,
and I was back from college
for the summer and Robert
was away, Mother didn't say
anything. We watched
the sky turn dark and light again
and we put on masks
when we went in to see him,
washed everything
the nurses were afraid of.
I guess we'll be all right,
Dad said, when he'd fought it off.
The doctors, amazed, wrote him
up for possible future
strategic maneuvers.
They studied him like a map.

Then when mother
got cancer, and I was away,
Robert stayed, doing the dishes
and rearranging the cupboards
while he kept an eye on Dad.
After the plateware,
Robert filed the soup
and the crackers
in neat rows for reference
in ascending order of taste.
He said, when I called
frantic from Kansas
after the third surgery:

It's like a war I guess,
but as long as we keep
track of each other
and calm,
we'll be all right.
He said:
The two of us learned
early, you know, to do that.

MUSING ON FLOWER POEMS

(muse comes from a word meaning
"to stand with an open mouth")

Such roses may come out!
Such thick thorns and scented petals
blooming out of our tongues—
it's hard to close the lips—
even mulch can keep the jaw slack
and the pen sifting, a pause
here and there for the pruning shears,
the show judges, the occasional
problem with aphids. But such
fragrant sounds: like spring.

So we stand with our mouths open
like fools, making our puns and gestures
till a garden comes twisting out, all wild
at first, maybe just budding—
we lick and kiss it, breathing
it back into lungs and out again
till the petals open and each is framed
by green. Roses rest like pendants
around our collar bones and shoulders,
like a knitted shawl of words that scratch
and blossom. Shoots wind back in.

The fingers we use to place the vases
are sprouting. If we gape long enough,
the whole body turns to summer.

Index

In this index, the entries in boldface type are poets' names, the entries in quotation marks are titles of poems, and all other entries are first lines of poems.